# PRAISE FOR *CONSUMED BY HATE, REDEEMED BY LOVE*

"As a kid in Mississippi in the late 1960's, I remember the men of our church discussing the Klan's bombing campaign against the Jews. The men did not disapprove. Later, I would use this fascinating chapter of civil rights history as the backdrop for my novel, *The Chamber*. Now, one of the bombers, Thomas Tarrants tells the real story in this remarkable memoir. It is riveting, inspiring, at times hard to believe but utterly true, and it gives some measure of hope in these rancorous times."
　　—JOHN GRISHAM

"The amazing story of how God delivered my friend Tom Tarrants from racism and hatred and gave him a heart of love and friendship for people of all colors and backgrounds. This book gives hope for what God can do."
　　—DR. JOHN PERKINS, PRESIDENT EMERITUS OF THE JOHN
　　　PERKINS FOUNDATION AND COFOUNDER EMERITUS OF THE
　　　CHRISTIAN COMMUNITY DEVELOPMENT ASSOCIATION

"This gripping and inspiring story is as timely as today's headlines. My friend Tom Tarrants is a trophy of God's grace—and testament to how God not only changes our eternity but can transform our hearts and minds for today. So put on your seatbelt and prepare to enter into one of the most extraordinary true stories you'll ever encounter!"
　　—LEE STROBEL, BESTSELLING AUTHOR OF *THE
　　　CASE FOR CHRIST* AND *THE CASE FOR GRACE*

"Most of us have never been part of a racist domestic terrorist cell. For all of us, though, the story of this book is our story. We were, all of us, alienated from God and hiding from him behind something, whether white supremacist hatred or career advancement, sexual promiscuity or self-righteous religion. The same Christ confronts all of us, and the same gospel can transform. This book, of the transition from a Ku Klux Klansman to a gospel Christian, is a riveting narrative. You will be gripped by the story and, I hope, by the Story behind the story. This is the path from burning crosses to the cross of Christ himself, from raging hate to amazing grace. How I love that story. You will too."
　　—RUSSELL MOORE, PRESIDENT OF THE ETHICS AND RELIGIOUS
　　　LIBERTY COMMISSION OF THE SOUTHERN BAPTIST CONVENTION

"The dramatic story of Tom Tarrants's conversion from terrorist to advocate for peace is simply astonishing. It is also essential reading for these times. If you want to understand how the evil of extremist thought works—and how the gospel of God's grace can overcome it—read this book."

—MARK BATTERSON, *NEW YORK TIMES* BESTSELLING
AUTHOR OF *THE CIRCLE MAKER* AND LEAD PASTOR
OF NATIONAL COMMUNITY CHURCH

"Reveals how easily a political ideology can grow into a radical, extreme, life-taking worldview, all the while masquerading as some supposed form of a 'Christian' faith. A powerful story!"

—ERIC C. REDMOND, ASSOCIATE PROFESSOR OF BIBLE
AT THE MOODY BIBLE INSTITUTE, CHICAGO

"A rivetingly told tale. Will America ever be free of its 'original sin' of racism? Tarrants goes on record against himself, shining the light on the dark workings of his own radicalization as a domestic terrorist. But in showing how grace and forgiveness broke into his own life to give him a second chance, he points the way for all who strive to rid America of this terrible scourge and the hatred that it breeds."

—OS GUINNESS, AUTHOR OF *LAST CALL FOR LIBERTY*

"At a time when the blight of hatred, racial division, and tribalistic contempt spreads and seeps into our politics, communities, and churches, Tom Tarrants's extraordinary, often horrifying, and miraculous story offers both insight and instruction. He shows the ways in which hate warps the mind and corrupts the heart, as well as the allure of scapegoating and rigid ideology and the human carnage left in their wake. But this is ultimately a story of amazing grace—how one blinded by hate learned to see, to love, and to reconcile. And it offers hope, showing the possibilities for the flowering of such grace, even on the cultural battlefields of our own riven land."

—CHERIE HARDER, PRESIDENT OF THE
TRINITY FORUM, WASHINGTON, DC

"When I met Tom Tarrants at Parchman prison so many years ago, I sensed him as a pleasant, well-mannered, and intelligent man. I wondered why he was there. I did not have any sense of how our lives would intersect. Only later did I learn the depths to which the demons of racism had driven him. This riveting story of a journey from darkness into light is about the total renovation that God's grace can bring about—of mind, heart, and soul. What impresses me as much as Tom's initial journey into faith is his renouncing the temptations of celebrity status and desire to live as a humble disciple of Jesus, quietly guiding others on the same path. This is a needed story for our time."

—LEIGHTON FORD, PRESIDENT OF LEIGHTON FORD MINISTRIES

"From racism to reconciliation. From Klan-inspired hatred to passionate love with understanding. Tom Tarrants's story and reflections show that there is hope for our times, even in the midst of rancor and division. This is a must-read for the church in America!"

—DENNIS P. HOLLINGER, PHD, PRESIDENT AND
COLMAN M. MOCKLER DISTINGUISHED PROFESSOR OF
CHRISTIAN ETHICS, GORDON-CONWELL SEMINARY

CONSUMED
redeemed
BY
HATE
love

# CONSUMED
## redeemed
# BY
## by
# HATE
## love

How a Violent Klansman Became a
Champion for Racial Reconciliation

THOMAS A. TARRANTS

NELSON
BOOKS

An Imprint of Thomas Nelson

Published in Nashville, Tennessee, by Nelson Books, an imprint of Thomas Nelson. Nelson Books and Thomas Nelson are registered trademarks of HarperCollins Christian Publishing, Inc.

Published in association with the literary agency of Wolgemuth & Associates, Inc.

Thomas Nelson titles may be purchased in bulk for educational, business, fund-raising, or sales promotional use. For information, please e-mail SpecialMarkets@ThomasNelson.com.

Unless otherwise noted, Scripture quotations are taken from the ESV® Bible (The Holy Bible, English Standard Version®). Copyright © 2001 by Crossway, a publishing ministry of Good News Publishers. Used by permission. All rights reserved.

Scripture quotations marked NIV are from the Holy Bible, New International Version®, NIV®. Copyright © 1973, 1978, 1984, 2011 by Biblica, Inc.® Used by permission of Zondervan. All rights reserved worldwide. www.Zondervan.com. The "NIV" and "New International Version" are trademarks registered in the United States Patent and Trademark Office by Biblica, Inc.®

Any Internet addresses, phone numbers, or company or product information printed in this book are offered as a resource and are not intended in any way to be or to imply an endorsement by Thomas Nelson, nor does Thomas Nelson vouch for the existence, content, or services of these sites, phone numbers, companies, or products beyond the life of this book.

ISBN 978-1-4002-1533-1 (eBook)
ISBN 978-1-4002-1532-4 (HC)

**Library of Congress Control Number: 2019938090**

*Printed in the United States of America*
19 20 21 22 23  LSC  10 9 8 7 6 5 4 3 2 1

*All author royalties have been directed to
the National Christian Foundation for
the support of evangelism, discipleship,
reconciliation, and mercy ministries.*

# CONTENTS

# INTRODUCTION

About fifteen years ago, former White House aide and Watergate figure Chuck Colson said to me, "You *must* get your life story back
in print." He was referring to a book I had written in the late 1970s that
described the events of my life up to that point. It was an account of God's
grace and love to me when I was a hate-filled terrorist, and of how he
miraculously spared my life on two occasions and brought me to faith
in his Son. Chuck and I had been friends for many years, so I listened
politely, but the idea didn't resonate with me. I had had enough publicity
to last two lifetimes, and the last thing I wanted was more.

But in the years following Chuck's exhortation, at least half a dozen
people who didn't know one another said essentially the same thing to
me, leading me to conclude that God might be trying to send me a message. So, after much prayer and reflection, I set out to revise the original
book and update it to cover some of God's additional workings in my life
during the forty years since 1976, the last year the earlier book covered.
Cardiac and neurological issues along the way slowed the process, but
exceptional medical treatment and the prayers of my family and friends
enabled me to complete the writing.*

---

\* At the request of my family, for which my past notoriety has not been helpful, I have not
mentioned them in this book.

However, as I was finishing the book and exploring publishers, I began to see a significant resurgence of the racism, anti-Semitism, and political extremism that I had been a part of during the turbulent 1960s. This set off alarm bells in me not only for the societal impact but also for its seductive potential for some in the church. So, I decided to revise the book to be both an account of personal conversion and transformation and a cautionary tale for Christians today. It is also a story of hope. And yes, no matter what we may face in life, there is hope—hope in a loving and all-powerful God, for whom nothing is impossible.

The chapters ahead give a vivid and gripping account of how, in a period with similarities to our own, I was seduced by extremist ideology, became a terrorist, and in prison had a life-changing encounter with Jesus Christ that took me in a very different direction. The book concludes with a brief look at three elements of America's current social upheaval and suggestions about how to avoid becoming ensnared and respond in a way that glorifies God.

# Part 1

# SEEING GOD WORK IN THE EXTRAORDINARY

1968–1976

# AMBUSHED!

On a miserably hot and humid Mississippi afternoon, June 29, 1968, Kathy Ainsworth and I met over dinner to discuss our plan to bomb the house of a prominent Jewish leader in Meridian, Mississippi. We had been introduced a couple of years earlier and were both dedicated to "the Cause"—the cause of preserving America and white supremacy. This meant fighting against the civil rights movement, the liberals, and the Communist-Jewish conspiracy that was trying to destroy our nation. We saw ourselves as patriots, fighting for God and country. Neither of us had any idea of what awaited us just a few hours later.

Meyer Davidson was a wealthy, successful businessman in what was then a city of some forty thousand people. Several weeks earlier he had spoken out with great indignation after the bombing of Meridian's Jewish synagogue, Temple Beth Israel. Davidson publicly attacked Mississippi's White Knights of the Ku Klux Klan, described by the FBI as the most violent right-wing terrorist organization in the United States. He denounced its members, calling them maniacs. He also launched a fund-raising drive that raised $80,000 in reward money for information leading to the arrest and conviction of those responsible for the temple bombing.

Even though I wasn't an official member of the Mississippi Klan, I might as well have been. I had good friends who were, and I shared their views and concerns. Davidson's denunciation infuriated all of us. Such a public attack and aggressive action against the Klan would have been sufficient provocation for a violent response. But other, more practical considerations had also influenced the decision to bomb his house and my readiness to be part of the plot.

Since mid-January that year, Klansmen in Meridian had conducted a reign of terror that garnered attention all the way to Washington, DC. They had firebombed or burned eight black churches and three homes (two black families and one white family). This was part of a larger terror campaign that had been going on for several months in Mississippi. FBI director J. Edgar Hoover had ordered his organization to put a stop to it. A large number of federal agents were at work in Mississippi, assisted by state and local law enforcement agencies. Their initial efforts focused chiefly on Klansmen brothers Wayne and Raymond Roberts. Wayne had been recently convicted in the murders of James Earl Chaney, Andrew Goodman, and Michael Schwerner, three civil rights workers who had been abducted in Philadelphia, Mississippi, in 1964. Even though Wayne was identified as the triggerman in those crimes, he was free on bond while his case was on appeal.

The Roberts brothers had been able to handle the pressure until the bombing of Temple Beth Israel and the national outcry following the Meyer Davidson news coverage. At that point, the Mississippi Public Safety commissioner sent a special group of state investigators, known as "the goon squad," to Meridian to assist local police in pressuring the two men into cooperating. In an effort to cause them either to talk or make a mistake, this special squad followed them everywhere, watching their homes around the clock, visiting their workplaces, and in an interesting role reversal, quietly threatening the Klansmen's lives.

The pressure soon took its toll. In mid-June Raymond Roberts went to Jackson several times to ask one of my friends for help. About a week later, my friend traveled to Meridian for further discussions with both Raymond and Wayne. They decided that something had to be done to relieve the pressure from law enforcement, and soon. They concluded the best thing would be yet another major act of violence against Jews, one consistent with the ongoing campaign of terror to make the act appear to be the work of those who bombed the synagogue. This time, however, the Roberts brothers, knowing in advance of the bombing, would have an airtight alibi—being seen publicly elsewhere with many witnesses. In theory, the focus of the investigation—and the harassment—would shift away from them.

Though I was not in Mississippi while these discussions were taking place, the choice of Meyer Davidson as the target was at least partly my doing. After his public comments about the Temple Beth Israel bombing, I had mentioned to other Klansmen that Meyer Davidson, because of his profile, would be a good target for some future operation. I saw it as a good opportunity to demonstrate what could happen to those who brazenly attacked the Klan. And it would also more generally send a message to Jews, who we believed were behind the civil rights movement. When I returned to the state and learned of the pressure being applied to the Roberts brothers, I decided to be one of two bombers for this attack, which was planned for a few days later at the end of June. Time was of the essence, the Roberts brothers said, because a grand jury was meeting soon and would probably indict them.

But my prospective partner in the operation was a well-known Klansman, and whenever a major act of racial violence occurred, the FBI went straight to his house to see if he was home. To avoid compromising the operation and to relieve some of the pressure on him, at the last minute I suggested that he not go. That way he, like the Roberts brothers, would have an alibi when the bomb exploded and could greet the FBI when they came knocking on his door minutes later.

The only person who could replace him was Kathy Ainsworth, a trusted member of the Klan's inner circle in Jackson. Kathy was a smart, attractive brunette in her midtwenties who taught at a local elementary school and was not on the FBI's radar. Few people would have suspected her of Klan activities, as women were rarely involved in such things. She was proficient in intelligence gathering, clandestine operations, and the use of firearms. More important, she had experience in previous bombings. I drove to Kathy's house in Jackson to explain the situation to her.

When I arrived, Kathy was preparing to make the long, hot drive to her hometown of Miami for vacation. Her husband, Ralph, who knew nothing of her terrorist activities, was away at a two-week National Guard training camp. I described the plan for the Davidson attack, explaining the need to replace my prospective partner, and asked, "Can you go with me on this mission? If so, we can drop off the bomb in Meridian, and then I will drive you on to Miami."

"Yes, I can do it," she said without hesitation. "And I can introduce you to some patriots down there."

From my study of covert operations, I had learned that secrecy was the single most important factor in the success of terrorist activities. Information had to be tightly controlled and dispersed strictly on a need-to-know basis. Anyone not directly involved with an operation could not know about it. But in this case, that principle was not being followed. Although they would not be participating, both Raymond and Wayne Roberts knew the details of the operation. They were Klansmen—active terrorists themselves in the Meridian area. Part of the reason for this operation was to divert attention away from them. If anyone could be trusted, it was these two—or so I thought.

Kathy and I left Jackson and headed east toward Meridian. During the two-hour drive, we discussed our plan further. The bomb was set to detonate at 2:00 a.m. It consisted of twenty-nine sticks of dynamite and a separate, battery-powered timing device. It would do massive damage. By the time it exploded, we would be well on our way to Mobile. Kathy would spend the night with friends there before we continued on to Miami. I reassured her, "It will be a simple operation."

We reached the Meridian area at about eleven o'clock, stopping at a pay phone near a hamburger stand on the highway. I was all business now. "I'll call Raymond and be back in just a minute," I informed Kathy as I stepped out of the car.

I was now much more alert, and nervous tension was growing. Off in the darkness, a dog barked. The chirps of crickets and squeaks of tree frogs cascaded through the tall trees. The light from the phone booth dimmed my night vision, blinding me to all but the most overt surveillance that might be nearby. But that didn't matter; this wouldn't take long.

The restaurant was closed, the night was dark, and the air hung heavy with humidity.

I dropped my dime in the slot and dialed Raymond's number. He was expecting the call. We spoke only a few words, in code, signaling a meeting at a prearranged rendezvous point—a truck stop near Meridian.

"Is Bill there?" I asked.

"You've got the wrong number," he replied.

That was it. We assumed the presence of FBI wiretaps on our telephones. Therefore, we routinely employed countermeasures, such as the use of codes, veiled references, voice disguises, and especially short calls. This one had taken less than a minute.

I returned to the big Buick. It had bench seats and a powerful engine that made it fast—fast enough to outrun many police cruisers. Kathy and I drove in alert silence to the designated meeting place, a truck stop closer to town, where we waited in the parking lot.

Within a few minutes Raymond drove up. He came over to our car and got in the backseat, expecting to see me and another Klansman. Surprised at the presence of a woman, he demanded, "What's she doing here?"

"Don't worry," I replied. "She's been on missions like this before. She can do anything you can do and more."

After we talked for a few minutes, Raymond returned to his car. Kathy and I followed him to the nearby Holiday Inn, which had a late-night bar. Raymond parked his car and then got in the Buick with us to check out the Davidson house.

Meyer Davidson lived in an affluent, but not ostentatious, neighborhood. His house was a comfortable, ranch-style brick structure with a double carport, standing on a spacious, tree-shaded corner lot. Kathy, Raymond, and I circled his block twice and drove through the surrounding neighborhood, looking for anything that might indicate surveillance or the presence of a stakeout. Except for an occasional streetlight, the streets were quiet and dark—optimum conditions. I hadn't seen any problems and had no reason to expect any. I was nevertheless feeling tense and uneasy.

I knew that if anything went wrong, it could be disastrous. Because of the recent bombings and church burnings, tensions were high in Meridian. The police were in a heightened state of alert and under intense pressure from Chief Roy Gunn, a strong, domineering man with a temper, who was given to emotional outbursts and could be ruthless in achieving his goals. He was on a personal campaign to stop Klan violence in his city, no matter what it took, and he expected his officers to do whatever was necessary, legal or otherwise.

We drove back to the Holiday Inn and dropped off Raymond. It was now midnight. When the bomb exploded, he would have been in the bar for two hours with plenty of witnesses. We continued out to a secluded, wooded area several miles north of Meridian. There I retrieved the bomb from the trunk of the car.

With no witnesses other than the stars and the deepening darkness, in the dim glow of the trunk light, I connected the electrical detonator to the dynamite and set the timer for 2:00 a.m. I got back in the car and gently placed the bomb on the front seat between Kathy and me. I looked at her and asked, "Are you ready?"

Kathy looked down at the bomb, then replied with an almost imperceptible hesitation, "Yes."

We headed back into Meridian. As we turned south onto Davidson's street, we saw his house ever so softly cast in the pale-yellow light of the lone streetlamp. It was a scene of tranquility that would soon be shattered.

I slowed to a stop about fifty feet from the drive leading to Davidson's residence. It was almost 1:00 a.m. As near as we could tell, the entire neighborhood was asleep. The house was set back about forty feet from the street. On our left, directly across the street, was a five-foot embankment with trees and shrubbery that partially obscured a neighboring house from view. The embankment would shield that house from a large part of the bomb's blast.

Ever so quietly, I opened the car door and stepped out in the dimly lit street. The humid night air once again enveloped me. Kathy remained in the car. I tucked a pistol into the waistband of my trousers, then lifted the bomb from the front seat and cradled it. I gently closed the car door behind me. Any sound it made was drowned out by the cacophony of chirping crickets.

Full of tension, I walked silently around the front of my car and up the concrete driveway. I was almost there.

Then a gunshot pierced the night. And a man shouted.

More gunshots boomed. The bullets made whizzing pops as they passed me.

They seemed to come from every direction.

And they were all aimed at me.

I dropped the bomb, which should have exploded instantly but didn't. As I spun around and ran back to the car, the pistol in my waistband spun out and fell to the ground, unfired.

I had to reach the car.

I had to get away.

My mind began to race: *Did Davidson see us? Where are all the shots coming from?* We had to get away before police sealed off the area.

As I reached the front of the Buick, a hot, massive blast tore through my upper right leg. It was buckshot. The force of the impact stunned me. I grabbed the hood of the car to keep from collapsing. I didn't see the shooter, but he couldn't have been more than twenty feet away.

I was hit. I sensed pain that my amped-up mind didn't fully register. But I did fully register the continuing bangs and booms of gunfire. Bullets and buckshot were flying everywhere around me. Inexplicably, although I was completely exposed to the barrage, I was not hit again.

Once more I strained forward, on a wounded and wobbly right leg, lurching toward the driver's door. Kathy leaned over from the passenger side to open it and pull me in.

Hot lead now tore through the heavy metal of the big Buick. The concealed shooters were pumping round after round of rifle and shotgun fire into the car.

I started the engine, dropped the car into gear, floored the accelerator, and sped away through the hail of gunfire. I could feel the warm blood flowing out of my leg and onto the front seat.

As I sped down the street, I heard Kathy say in a soft voice, "Tommy, I've been hit." I took a quick glance over at her. In the yellow glow of a passing streetlight, I saw a bullet hole at the base of her neck.

"I've been hit, too, Kathy, but we're going to make it. Don't worry. There's a doctor in Jackson who can help us."

When she didn't reply, I looked over again and saw her body slumped over on the seat.

I was careening south down Twenty-Ninth Street, toward the highway to Jackson. It looked as though we might get away. I experienced a bright moment of hope that both Kathy and I could find medical help and survive this night's disaster.

Seemingly out of nowhere, a police car zoomed up behind us. Its driver practically fastened his vehicle onto our rear bumper. I would later learn that it was a brand-new Ford Police Interceptor with a more powerful engine than the Buick's. I glanced up in my rearview mirror and saw an officer hanging out the passenger window, aiming a shotgun.

*Boom! Boom!*

The rear windshield shattered. I swerved to throw off the shooter's aim until he had to reload. I made a hard right at the next intersection, then another. But in that kind of turning chase, the Buick was no match for the lighter and nimbler Ford. The police car stayed right on my bumper, pumping round after round into the car. Once again, inexplicably, I was not hit.

In a last desperate effort, I turned again, this time to the left, putting the shooter on the outside of the turn. But I had taken the turn too fast and skidded to the right and off the paved street. With the big engine screaming, we smashed up and over the curb, coming to a rest half in the street and half in the yard of a corner house. The police cruiser was so close behind that it couldn't stop, and it crashed into the rear of the Buick.

For a moment there was silence. The smell of hot brakes and smoking motor oil and burned rubber wafted through the hot, muggy air.

But I wasn't done yet.

More reacting than thinking, I grabbed my submachine gun from under the front seat and jumped out of the car. The cop in the passenger seat of the police car had jumped out of his door, brandishing a shotgun, but I had been faster. I fired a sustained burst, spraying the stream of bullets between the two cops. The cruiser's windshield was destroyed. At least three rounds struck the first cop in the chest, and he went down.

The driver, his partner, dove beneath the dashboard, and my burst missed him entirely.

My ammunition magazine was empty, and the spares were in the car, so I dropped the empty submachine to the pavement. Suddenly, the driver stood up and fired a shotgun blast, striking me in the upper left leg and abdomen. But instead of firing again and killing me, the officer stepped back into his car.

Somehow, I managed to stagger away. I made my way to the backyard of an adjacent house, where some shrubbery partially concealed me. I tried to scale the chain-link fence, but it was topped with a strand of electrified wire. It delivered a surprisingly powerful electric shock that knocked me to the ground. Stunned, I tried to get up. I couldn't. My strength was gone. All I could do was lie in the shrubbery where I fell and hope I was hidden enough that the cops wouldn't find me.

A sensation of creeping numbness inched over me—as if I were in a rowboat drifting slowly into a foggy night. Somewhere out in the fog I could hear sirens. They seemed to be coming in from every direction. People shouting. Dogs barking. Police officers fanning out with their big, powerful flashlights.

A beam fell on me.

"Here he is, in the bushes," said a voice from behind the flashlight.

Four armed men approached me with great caution, holding their lights on me each step of the way. I lay very still, with my eyes closed, lest some movement cause one of them to shoot. I heard footsteps stop a few feet away. Then the lights went out.

A moment of silence, then *Boom! Boom! Boom! Boom!*

Four deafening shotgun blasts in rapid succession. Two loads of buckshot ripped into my right arm just below the elbow, nearly tearing it off. The other two hit the ground a mere inch or two short, kicking up dirt on my chest. I knew my right arm was shattered. And I was surprised I wasn't dead.

There was another pause in the fighting, but unlike earlier, this time I was quite done.

A flashlight beam shone directly in my face. I squinted against its piercing brilliance. A voice from beyond the beam asked, "Is he dead?"

A strong hand fastened around my wrist and began dragging me out of the bushes. A voice swore, "No, the son of a bitch is still alive." The orders from Police Chief Roy Gunn had been "drop them," no survivors. For the fourth time that night, I was at death's door.

Just then, another man came running up. It was an ambulance driver. Had he arrived a few seconds later, the officer with the pistol would have already fired the kill shot. But with a witness—a civilian witness—he couldn't risk pulling the trigger.

The police officers all shouldered or holstered their weapons. Without another word, they put me on a stretcher and carried me to a waiting ambulance, where Kathy had already been carried. They placed my stretcher next to hers, an FBI agent climbed in, and they slammed the door closed. The ambulance driver exchanged a few brief words with the attendant, turned on the siren, and began the race to Meridian's Matty Hersee Hospital.

Hovering over me, the attendant saw how dire my situation was. I could feel the blood seeping out of my wounds. I tried to speak, but no sound came out.

"The girl is dead," he said.

I closed my eyes. Bloody and battered, I was slipping deeper into the fog.

I remember hearing the siren. But that was all. I couldn't think or feel emotion.

When we reached Matty Hersee Hospital, I opened my eyes, but just barely. Everything was blurry. I could dimly make out police cars and people waiting for me at the emergency entrance. It seemed as if police were everywhere.

As soon as the ambulance team wheeled me into the emergency room, nurses and doctors cut away my blood-soaked clothes. I lay naked while they swabbed me and inserted probes into the bullet holes to determine the extent of my injuries.

Standing right behind the doctors, uniformed police and FBI agents looked on. I was captured and helpless while my enemies gazed down on me with contempt. It was like a scene from my worst nightmare.

I don't know how long I lay there, but my mind began to drift. I couldn't recall how I had come to be there.

My mouth was as dry as a sunbaked salt flat.

"We can't give you anything right now," said a nurse.

At last the nurse placed a few small shavings of ice on my tongue. The relief was incredible.

Meanwhile a swarm of ER nurses buzzed about, prepping me for a surgery that no one expected me to survive. For some reason they were holding off on administering the merciful anesthetic that would render me oblivious to my condition.

Suddenly the nurses were gone, and what seemed like a squad of federal agents circled the metal examination table. "You're not going to make it," one said. "Why don't you make a confession and get all your crimes off your conscience before you die?"

The emergency room doctor had taken one look at my wounds and estimated I had perhaps forty-five minutes to live. These agents wanted me to deal a death blow to the Klan by linking the bombing to KKK imperial wizard Sam Bowers and revealing the identities of my accomplices. But faithful to the Cause and the Ku Klux Klan's code of secrecy, I told them nothing—not that I could have said a lot, even if I had wanted to. I could barely speak. Then, just as suddenly as they came, they disappeared.

The Matty Hersee operating room was a dingy, old-fashioned place where a single klieg light overhead shone directly into my eyes. It smelled like Lysol and rubbing alcohol. A masked nurse fiddled with the IV drip in my arm and said, "Start counting backwards from one hundred."

"Ninety-nine, ninety-eight . . ."

And then I was blissfully, blessedly unconscious.

# 2 AN UNDESERVED MERCY

The surgery to save my life began at about 2:30 Sunday morning and continued for several hours. During that time, my life hung by a thread. Somehow the surgical team had stanched the bleeding and mitigated the worst of the gunshot damage. But the damage to my body was extensive. There was the open question of how and whether to repair it.

I remained sedated for a long time afterward. Slowly, imperceptibly, I began to wake up. I first heard the nurses moving about, monitoring my vital signs and checking the circulation in my wounded right arm. I opened my eyes just a little. I struggled to focus. The first thing I noticed was that, like the operating room, this room was old and dingy. The next thing I noticed was an IV needle lodged in my left arm. It hurt. A lot.

Sometime later, a uniformed police officer escorted my mother, father, and girlfriend into the room. It was an extremely emotional reunion. They had made the long drive from Mobile, Alabama, where they lived. My mom was crying. So was my girlfriend. My dad looked like he was carrying the weight of the whole world on his shoulders, and his eyes welled with tears. The three of them stood around my bed, each trying to touch me someplace I hadn't been wounded.

Over and over, they assured me of their love. They promised to stand by me no matter what. They promised to get me the best possible medical treatment. The near-certain prospect of my going to prison was never uttered. It felt so good to see them—to feel their love, their touch—even if only for a minute or two. I've never needed human love as much as I did right then.

Overcome with emotion, I summoned the strength to speak. "Mama, Daddy, I'm sorry . . . to do this . . . to you . . . but I had . . . to fight . . . for the Cause." Then I sank back into unconsciousness, leaving them to face what I had become and done—and to face all of the publicity, which had spread like wildfire across America and beyond by television, radio, and newspapers.

When I woke up, they were gone. A nurse came in to check on me. Heavily armed law enforcement officers stood guard outside the door of my room. After watching them for a while, I got the distinct feeling they cared little whether I lived or died. Surely some preferred the latter.

The shotgun blasts that ended the gunfight the night before had mangled my right arm. The emergency surgical team had cleaned out the gaping wound, removing bone fragments and splinters. A four-inch section of my ulna bone just below the elbow had been completely blown away. The surgeons had initially considered amputating my arm. However, there was a slight chance of saving it with the help of an exceptionally skilled orthopedic surgeon.

Fortunately for me at that time, Meridian, Mississippi, was home to one of the best orthopedic surgeons in the United States. Dr. Leslie Rush, the man who headed Rush Foundation Hospital in Meridian, was a pioneer in the design and manufacture of the first generation of stainless-steel pins and screws for traumatic bone repair.

My parents went straight to see him. After coming over and examining me, Dr. Rush agreed to treat me pro bono. On July 2, 1968, three days after my capture, a large, heavily armed police convoy transported me from Matty Hersee Hospital directly to an operating suite at the Rush Foundation Hospital. Police were everywhere. They surrounded the building, guarded every entrance, and patrolled the corridors and stairwells inside the building.

As I was being prepared for surgery at the Rush Foundation Hospital, I considered myself extremely fortunate. For starters, I was alive. Plus, I was about to have my shattered arm fixed by one of the best surgeons in the country—for free. Although I was a prisoner, I was being held in far better conditions—at least for the moment—than I would have dared to hope. I was young and I was clever. And one day I would be strong again, strong enough to escape. Freedom beckoned. So did the Cause.

The last thing I remember is the anesthesiologist asking me to count backward from one hundred.

"Ninety-nine, ninety-eight . . ."

The facilities at Rush were much better than at Matty Hersee. After surgery the orderlies wheeled me into a private room—at a time when most hospital inpatients were doubled up in smaller rooms. That part of the floor was designated off-limits to all but members of the massive police garrison and a few select doctors and nurses. Police officers stood watch in my room and in the hall outside around the clock. Other officers waited in the room across the hall. No one was going to get close to me without passing a screen of Meridian police.

\*     \*     \*

While I was in surgery at Rush Hospital, Kathy Ainsworth was being buried in Magee, Mississippi, a sleepy little town about halfway between Jackson and Hattiesburg. I had asked my parents to send a large spray of flowers to her funeral, and they did. Against her husband Ralph's wishes, the Ku Klux Klan had turned out in full strength wearing their signature white robes, memorializing her as a martyr. In full sympathy with the Klan, Kathy's mother described her as a martyr for the Cause.

Kathy was raised in Florida and attended Coral Gables High School, graduating with honors. She babysat often for Adon Taft, the religion editor of the *Miami Herald* newspaper, whose family loved her and thought she was the ideal example of a young woman. Kathy went on to attend Mississippi College, a Baptist school in Jackson, Mississippi.

At the time of her death, Kathy was teaching fifth grade at the Lorena Duling elementary school in Jackson. She was loved by her husband, her students, and their parents, and was well respected in her community. Her Klan involvement and death under such circumstances was a shock that sent her students and their parents into heartbreaking bewilderment and disorientation. How could such a kind, genteel schoolteacher also be a secret terrorist? They could not reconcile the Kathy they knew with the person they discovered she was.

*    *    *

When I awoke from surgery, I discovered another IV drip in my left arm. My immobilized and heavily bandaged right arm was searing with an unrelenting, sharp pain even worse than before.

A nurse came and delivered a dose of narcotic mercy that quickly returned me to painless and peaceful unconsciousness.

It was the first of many such shots.

For the first few days at Rush Hospital, I was fed intravenously and kept heavily sedated. I was given regular injections of Demerol, a potent painkiller. Gradually, however, I developed a tolerance to it, which meant increasing the size or frequency of the dose—and the risk of addiction. My doctors decided against increasing my dosage. For more than two weeks, I endured excruciating pain in my right arm. This was aggravated and amplified by the awkward and uncomfortable position in which I had to lie. Night after night I suffered through agonizing hours of intermittent sleep and intense, throbbing pain.

Nonetheless, the hours turned into days, and my condition stabilized. The IV drips were disconnected. I began eating solid food again. I quickly learned to write and eat with my left hand. Until then it had never occurred to me that I would have so much appreciation for such a simple pleasure as eating. And what a good feeling it was when the orderly shaved me each morning!

I gained strength with each passing day, and despite the horrible wounds in both my legs, the nurses were soon walking me around the room and down the hall. "The danger of blood clots or pneumonia far outweighs the risk of getting up and walking a little each day," they said. With a nurse on each arm, I took my first, short, unsteady steps toward recovery. The unspoken question was, recovery to what?

\*     \*     \*

During my time at Rush, the only visitors I was allowed were members of my immediate family. My father and mother, though separated at the time, worked together and came to see me as often as police would permit—almost daily at first. My brother, sister, grandmother, and girlfriend faithfully accompanied my family on the many trips but were made to wait downstairs and rarely got to see me. I was amazed at their love and support. How could they still love me in light of all that I had done? I had ignored my family's warnings about getting involved with extremists and as a result had brought shame and disgrace on our entire family. That was a big deal in a traditional Southern town like Mobile. But that didn't matter to them now. There was no finger-pointing, no saying "I told you so." Far from disowning me, they were doing everything they could to help me, at great personal and financial expense. Their love was healing.

One afternoon about ten days after my transfer to Rush, I received a surprising visitor. In a major exception to the no-visitor policy, an attorney from Laurel, Mississippi, was permitted to visit with me. Percy Quinn had been sent by Sam Bowers, imperial wizard of the Ku Klux Klan, to see how I was doing, to reassure me of Klan support, and to learn the details of the police ambush. Quinn was not the most sought-after of the Klan's roster of lawyers, which confirmed to me that my situation looked hopeless. But he offered to represent me and try to arrange bond. He later confided to my family that there was nothing he could do to get me released on bail.

A few days later, I was scheduled for more surgery on my arm.

Early on the morning of my surgery, a nurse woke me up for an injection. A few minutes later two orderlies came in and placed me on a gurney. At least half a dozen policemen with submachine guns and sawed-off shotguns surrounded me. They wheeled the gurney to the elevator and down to the operating suite. When we reached the operating room, where a number of other officers were waiting, my escorts seemed noticeably relieved.

The surgery went well, and in a couple of days I was back in my routine. Then, one morning, a couple of new nurses came to my room. They were physical therapists and had come to teach me how to exercise the fingers of my right hand. I obediently flexed and exercised my fingers several times a day. Little by little I regained near-normal use of my hand.

During those long days and nights of recovery, I read from a Gideon Bible that was on the bedside table, looking for encouragement, hope, and maybe some answers. But as I tried to read the New Testament, I found it difficult to understand, especially in the Elizabethan language of the King James Version. And the few verses I had used to justify hatred of Jews and blacks and my fight for "God and country" were of scant comfort. So I gave it up and concentrated on getting answers to the questions that had most needled me since the ambush.

How had the police discovered our plan?

What had gone wrong?

Unlike other Klan groups, our team operated in a well-organized, sophisticated, professional way. We took the strictest security precautions. We had made only one exception—allowing the Roberts brothers to be part of the planning of the operation without being present for it.

Day after day, as I lay in bed with my eyes closed, I would catch snippets of conversation between the policemen guarding me. Sometimes the officers would discuss the incident with me. Overall, that was a mistake, because their comments and questions only succeeded in giving me clues about what they knew. It soon became clear that the Meridian Police Department had obtained considerable inside information on the Meyer Davidson operation. As I put the pieces together, it appeared that the Roberts brothers were the most likely source.

I also learned that around four thirty on the afternoon before the bombing attempt, someone had telephoned my grandmother, asking to speak to Thomas Tarrants III. He said he had to get in touch with me right away. My grandmother told him I wasn't there. The caller then asked if I had gone to Mississippi. My grandmother replied she didn't know where I was but that she would "give anything in this world to know." Like the rest of my family, she had not seen me for several months.

Before hanging up the phone, the caller emphasized, "I've got to get him right away!"

I'm sure someone had called to warn me of the ambush in Meridian. Was it someone on the Meridian Police Department? Or someone else who had learned of what was about to happen?

Then, toward the end of July, during my last week in Rush Hospital, a stranger in civilian clothes walked into my room and announced that he was Officer Mike Hatcher. Officer Hatcher was the police officer that I'd blasted with my submachine gun after he jumped out of his car. I hit him three times in the chest, once in the heart. He had undergone open-heart surgery that saved his life. Despite near-fatal wounds and the major surgery to repair them, he looked healthy and fit.

I didn't know what to say, so I asked, "How are you doing?"

"I'm fine," he said. "And I want to let you know that I'm a better man than you are." And then he left.

Since then I have wondered: What did that mean—his strength and stamina in surviving a more serious wound than mine? Or that he recovered before I did? Or maybe that the police had finally won?

About midmorning on August 2, after a month of hospitalization, Sheriff Alton Allen came to my room and said, "Gather up your stuff. You're going to jail."

# PAYING THE PRICE

The Lauderdale County Courthouse was a large, gray stone building five stories tall. It loomed over an entire city block in downtown Meridian, housing both the courtrooms and jail cells. I was about to become familiar with both.

The arrival of the transport convoy was quite a procession. Uniformed police had sealed off all traffic on the street in front. Policemen and highway patrolmen with shotguns and scoped high-power rifles lined the front of the courthouse and along the street as well. Handcuffed and clad in pajamas and a bathrobe, I limped toward the building, encircled by my heavily armed bodyguard.

Once inside the building, I was taken by elevator to the fourth floor. There I met Buck Lewis, the jailer. Jangling his big key ring, Mr. Lewis inserted a large key into a heavy steel door. It opened into a chamber about twenty feet wide by thirty feet long.

Solid concrete walls held three windows with thick, dirty glass and fat steel bars. In the middle of the chamber, running lengthwise, was a rectangular, steel dining table. A small shower stall with no curtain was in a corner. This "day room," as they called it, was where prisoners got out of their cells during the day to eat, sit around and talk, and play cards. Along the full length of one wall were four, four-man cells with sliding doors that opened into the day room. These cells were small—about seven by ten feet. Each cell had four bunks, stacked two high on either side, a face bowl, and a toilet just inside the sliding door. But all the cells were empty. I had the entire cellblock all to myself.

Mr. Lewis directed me into the first cell on my right and rolled the steel cell door shut behind me. Through the bars of my new cage, he handed me two clean sheets to cover the overused, filthy mattress on the steel bunk bed. Then, without another word, everyone filed out. The steel door to the cellblock banged shut with an imposing metallic thud.

Until this point, I had been kept in the antiseptic environment of a modern hospital. The police guards notwithstanding, I had been treated with dignity and care. I'd always had people around me. But the clanging of that cellblock door changed all that. Suddenly I was alone—totally alone. Isolated. I was in a dirty steel cage in a dirty, concrete room. In the dim light that passed through the dirty, steel-barred windows, I saw little hope for the future. The stark reality of my predicament was more than I could bear. For the first time since my arrest, I broke down. I wept uncontrollably.

For five years my life had centered on the Cause. I had passionately devoted myself to it, just as a man gives himself to his wife or his god. Indeed, for me the Cause had grown to be a god of sorts, as it dominated my thinking and my life. Everything was subordinate to it: family, career, relationships, reputation, and the varied pleasures of life. I lived for it. I sacrificed and suffered for it. If necessary, I was willing to die for it.

Captured and caged in a cell, I could no longer pursue the Cause, though I was as devoted as ever. My work would fall to others while I languished in prison. With everything I had built my life on now lost, my reason for existence began to disappear, along with my identity. I became very depressed. My life was over, or so it seemed. I could see no point in continuing. To die would be better than to live.

Because of the persistent pain from my injuries, I was given a daily oral dose of a powerful painkiller by the jailer, who didn't ensure that I actually swallowed it. A large enough dose would be fatal, and peacefully so. I decided to save up the pills and take them all at once. I reasoned that death would end my misery and open the way to heaven. In my youth I had prayed to accept Christ as my Savior and had been assured that I would go to heaven when I died. This belief had enabled me to face dangerous situations in the past without fear of death, and it was only natural that I would invoke it now.

One night, I took a handful of these pills, expecting to die. However, I eventually woke up in a daze, sick to my stomach, feeling terrible. Even worse, I was still alive. And I was still alone in the Lauderdale County Jail. No one even knew about my attempted suicide. Why I didn't die is a mystery, since this particular medication had been responsible for many deaths from overdoses. My depression only deepened. And there was no way out.

Life in jail was routine, bleak, and terribly, terribly boring. Breakfast was served around 6:00 a.m. and consisted of grits, biscuits, syrup, fried bologna, and an egg. Later in the morning, the jailer brought in a couple of prisoners who swept and mopped the cellblock. Lunch was the best meal of the day: good home-cooked Southern food and corn bread. Snacks and sodas were also available at a reasonable price for those who had money to pay. These activities might have taken an hour or so of the day.

My primary coping mechanism was sleep. I slept as much as possible. As long as I was asleep, I didn't have to face the misery of reality. When I wasn't sleeping, I would read. I turned to the Bible again, once again looking for encouragement or answers. The jailer had allowed me to have a King James Version Bible that my grandmother had given me. But half-way through the Old Testament, I became bored and laid it aside. It was rather dry reading, sometimes confusing, and didn't do anything for me. The only things left to read were the books and magazines that my parents brought me when they came to the jail on Wednesdays and Sundays, the two days prisoners were allowed to have visitors.

*      *      *

Several weeks after my transfer to the jail, two FBI agents came to visit me. Agents Frank Watts and Jack Rucker were warm, personable men, and for some reason I liked them—even though I hated the FBI at the time because it was fighting the Klan and other far-right groups. This was part of the FBI's Counterintelligence Program (COINTELPRO), originally set up in 1956 to counter Communist and socialist organizations in the United States, then expanded in the early 1960s to cover white hate groups and civil rights groups.

Their visit came as no surprise. I was in a position to supply a lot of information they wanted. My testimony could put certain people in prison for a long time. I could help them solve a number of cases they could not break, so it was only a matter of time until a couple of J. Edgar Hoover's agents would come calling. I knew what they wanted, and they knew I knew. Nevertheless, because I agreed to talk with them, we all pretended that cooperation was at least an option. A number of possibilities were discussed if I did. Money and a reduced sentence were among them. Also, the idea of serving whatever sentence I got at one of the low-security federal institutions, which would be like a country club compared to Mississippi's notorious Parchman prison, where I would probably be moved after my trial.

The truth was that my commitment to the Cause was undiminished, and I never had any intention of cooperating. No matter how miserable my present or future circumstances might be. I agreed to talk with them because they were likable guys, and I enjoyed matching wits with them. Had I known at the time what formidable opponents they were, I would have never agreed to talk with them. Frank's previous assignment in the bureau was compromising KGB agents in the Soviet delegation at the United Nations and turning them into double agents for the United States.

Frank was a good, moral man and church member. During the course of our talks, he realized how much my radical beliefs and behaviors had warped my view of God. Concerned about my spiritual condition, he asked his pastor at First Baptist Church in Meridian to come visit me. Of course, I saw nothing wrong with my views and was suspicious of his pastor's motives. Nothing we talked about changed my beliefs. However, I didn't know it at the time, but Frank's wife, Joyce, and the women in her prayer group were praying earnestly for me to be saved.

\*     \*     \*

My trial was scheduled for November 26, 1968. I was charged with attempting to place a bomb near a residence, which was a capital offense under Mississippi law. Charges for the attempted murder of Meridian police officer Mike Hatcher were not pressed. The authorities told me they knew I had committed other crimes, but they were only interested in trying me for the bombing charge, the most serious of all. It was enough: the death penalty (which they were seeking) or life in prison (which would guarantee that I would no longer be a threat to society). As I had been caught in the act by many eyewitnesses, I was sure to be convicted.

My family had retained Thomas Haas, a former assistant U.S. attorney from Mobile, to defend me. Tom was a good man and a fine lawyer. But I believed that his positions on race and civil rights issues were entirely too moderate, so I neither liked nor trusted him. My other attorney, Roy Pitts of Meridian, was also capable, although less experienced.

When Haas, a specialist in constitutional law, decided that my only defense was insanity, I was infuriated. He believed that anyone with views like mine had to be crazy. But the M'Naghten rule stated that I could not be found legally insane if I knew the difference between right and wrong at the time of the crime. By advancing the argument that radicals like me were insane by definition, Haas wanted to challenge and overthrow the M'Naghten rule. I would be his test case.

I viewed Haas's assertions as an insult to the Cause. They were in line with the rather common contention among our enemies in the liberal camp that people on the Far Right were sick or mentally ill. My consent to this defense would play into the hands of the enemy and make a mockery of all I believed in and had fought for. I refused to cooperate and demanded that he be fired. But my parents would hear nothing of this and continued to press me to cooperate with my lawyers. The impasse was broken when my girlfriend pleaded with me. She and I had lived together for a time and had considered marriage before I went underground several months earlier. For some reason, her appeals moved me when no others could, and I gave in.

Haas immediately called in a psychiatrist to examine me. After talking with my family, the psychiatrist, one of my mother's cousins, came to Meridian and talked with me in the jail for about forty-five minutes. After asking me a series of questions about who and where I was and why, he shifted to what I believed and how and when I had come to these convictions. I explained that I believed America was being undermined by Communists, socialists, liberals, and civil rights leaders who were influenced by a secret Jewish conspiracy intent on gaining control of the world. As a patriotic American, I saw it as my duty to fight it. On the basis of the information he gathered, he formed his opinion of my mental health.

Before the trial began, Haas was busy filing motions and laying out traps for the prosecution. Later he would use them to appeal the decision. The jury was composed of eleven white people and one black person.

The trial itself took only two days. The prosecution presented the overwhelming evidence of my guilt. In addition to weapons and explosives with my fingerprints all over them, half the Meridian police force had been eyewitnesses. When the prosecution rested, Tom Haas called my mother to the stand. She testified about the marked changes in my attitudes, values, and behavior as I became increasingly radicalized.

The psychiatrist was the key defense witness. He testified that in his opinion I was insane and should be given psychiatric treatment rather than sent to prison. In rebuttal, the prosecution called the director of the East Mississippi State Mental Hospital, also a psychiatrist. After reading my psychiatrist's report, he concluded that I might be emotionally disturbed, but I was not insane.

Dressed in a navy blue suit, I sat with my attorneys at the heavy oak defense table, taking in the proceedings attentively but disengaged emotionally and saying nothing. The courtroom was under tight security and full of law enforcement officers, reporters from various places, and other approved individuals, as well as my family. There was never any doubt that I would be convicted.

The case went to the jury late on the second day. After less than two hours of deliberation, they rendered their verdict. Standing beside my lawyers as stoically as I could, I listened as the jury foreman read aloud: "guilty of the capital offense of attempting to place a bomb near a residence."

They didn't buy the insanity plea.

The judge had three options in sentencing me: death, life in prison, or thirty years in prison. The prosecution had asked for the death penalty. Mississippi had a notorious and well-used gas chamber. However, in a ruling that surprised everybody, the judge sentenced me to thirty years in the Mississippi State Penitentiary, also known as Parchman prison.

Up until that moment, I hadn't dared to hope for any lenience. A death sentence wasn't just a real possibility; it had been the most likely outcome. But a thirty-year sentence was lenient indeed. I could be out in less than half that time with good behavior. If I didn't escape first.

I was then returned to my cell. Now, at last, it was over. I lay on my cell bunk and breathed several deep breaths. Gradually, the tensions of the previous months rolled off of me, and soon I was sound asleep.

# SEEDS OF FEAR AND ANGER

All of us are significantly shaped by the culture and times in which we grow up. In my case, a major part of the social environment that shaped me was the Southern culture in which I was raised. Like most white Southerners in those days, I embraced the history and conservative culture of the region, which had been passed down from family members, schooling, and the social structures of the time. Some of this was taught and some was "caught." Many Southerners had a sense of solidarity and pride in the memory of their ancestors who had "fought valiantly" in the Civil War, which some older people still referred to as the "War of Northern Aggression." Lingering resentment about the Reconstruction period, though fading, was also part of that legacy. People from the North often were viewed as outsiders and held at a distance socially. Black people, the vast majority of whom were not able to get a good education and typically had to work in low-status jobs, were considered by many whites as less intelligent and industrious than whites—and thus inferior.

Growing up in Mobile, I never knew anything but racial segregation. It was part of the fabric of life throughout the Southern states and always had been. It was what everyone grew up with, and the vast majority of white people considered it normal. All public facilities were segregated. Public restrooms, water fountains, and lunch counters all had signs labeled "White" or "Colored" so people would know which one to use. Restaurants, bars, clubs, buses, trains, schools, neighborhoods, and churches were all segregated. The unquestioned assumption among most whites was that they were superior to blacks and the two races must not be allowed to interact beyond certain set boundaries.

Having been born into the dominant side of this divided society, I never gave segregation a thought until federal mandates for school desegregation challenged it. Those challenges were very unsettling to me.

Born in 1946, I was a child of the 1950s. The United States was the most powerful country in the world. General Dwight D. Eisenhower, who had led the Allies to victory in World War II, was president, and widely popular. Churches were strong. The American middle class was growing out of the cities and into the suburbs. The national outlook was generally optimistic. Changes in society seemed beneficial, or at least benign: rock 'n' roll, Elvis, bigger and faster cars, rising hemlines, and a host of new consumer goods that were being marketed on a magic entertainment box called television. Most Americans remember the 1950s as a decade of domestic peace and prosperity.

It was also the decade of the family and a resurgence of religion. The Protestant evangelist Billy Graham and the Catholic bishop Fulton J. Sheen were popular and reaching large numbers of people. Churches were being built in the growing suburbs, and attendance was strong. I was a part of that. My mother made sure that my sister, brother, and I were in church every Sunday. At age thirteen I made a profession of faith and was baptized (though it had no effect on me).

But there were problems throughout that decade, and they portended change and challenge. During the first half of the decade, the forces of Communism were actively consolidating their gains from World War II. Then the Korean War erupted, intensifying the concern. During the second half of the decade, the Communists were busy expanding into the international political vacuum left by the collapse of the British and French empires.

America's preoccupation with domestic life emboldened the Communist regimes. Occasionally something would raise an alarm, such as the Army–McCarthy hearings, the discovery that Soviet spies had stolen America's nuclear secrets, the USSR's sudden development of the hydrogen bomb, Soviet suppression of the Hungarian uprising of 1956, or their surprising launch of the world's first satellite, Sputnik 1, in 1957. Still, for most people, American prosperity eclipsed these ominous developments.

Here at home, race relations and civil rights were gradually moving out of the shadows and into the national limelight. The 1954 Supreme Court ruling in *Brown v. Board of Education* was greatly encouraging to black Americans. But to many whites, especially in the South, it was deeply disturbing. That discomfort revealed itself in the infamous deseg-regation confrontation at Central High School in Little Rock, Arkansas, in September 1957, when Governor Orval Faubus, with widespread sup-port of segregationists, deployed the National Guard to block nine black students who were scheduled to enter under federal court order. President Eisenhower answered by sending in the army's famed 101st Airborne Division and federalizing the Arkansas National Guard. Newspaper pho-tos of the army at the school got my attention but didn't make much of an impression on me at the time.

Other race-related events were in the newspaper and on the tele-vision during that time as well. Rosa Parks's refusal to give up her seat on a city bus in Montgomery, Alabama, to a white person signaled the beginning of the Montgomery bus boycott, which gained national attention and became a major victory for the emerging civil rights movement. President Eisenhower went on to sign the Civil Rights Acts of 1957 and 1960, which provided federal protections for the rights of African American voters.

Throughout most of the 1950s, America looked and felt placid. And even if the placidity was superficial and illusory, that's how many white people like me remember it. Nevertheless, historic strategic and social shifts were already taking place, setting the stage for the turbulence of the next decade. Reality was about to shatter the illusion of the 1950s on a national scale, just as it would shake my personal life.

*        *        *

The culture and times I grew up in certainly shaped me, but family issues influenced me just as powerfully. By the early sixties I was a walking cauldron of anger and frustration, in part because of my relationship with my father and our dysfunctional home life.

My father was an intelligent, honest man, with an interest in history, politics, and current events. He worked in auto sales and management when I was young and in real estate when I was a teenager. Like many men in his occupation, he frequently worked until seven or eight in the evening. Unfortunately for my siblings and me, parenting was not one of his strengths. He loved us, but his work demanded and received the best part of his time. He didn't spend much personal time with me or my brother or sister. He frequently came home after supper, just before we were ready for bed. As I grew up, I would come to resent the order of his priorities.

Over time, alcohol became a big problem in my father's life. He was not violent or physically abusive, but the alcohol magnified his detachment and lengthened the emotional distance he already had from his family. I resented my alienation from him, and that resentment fed a growing anger. I hated the distance. I hated the silence. And I eventually came to hate him.

The strain in our relationship was further strained by the increasing tension between him and my mother, much of which concerned his drinking and its effects on our family. As I became more aware of the dynamic between them, I began to take my mother's side. Predictably, this turned distance into dispute between my father and me. We had a series of ugly confrontations, and I threatened him once.

Dad didn't know how to deal with me, so he stopped dealing with me altogether. That void became a vacuum. It set the stage for a lot of what followed, as it rendered me susceptible as a young man to the influence of those urging others to join the life-or-death cause of saving America, Christianity, and the white race.

The time I wasn't spending with my father left room for lots of other things. One of my favorite distractions was watching television. I liked movies about World War II, and there were lots of them on TV. I saw the United States as a great nation committed to good and fighting for freedom in the world. I was proud of my country and proud of her history. The film classics that reinforced these themes significantly shaped my thinking about America, patriotism, and my duty.

I also watched a lot of westerns, soaking up their classic portrayal of the struggle between good and evil. The scripts and the messages were mostly the same. The good guys, played by tall, rugged men, had to fight the bad guys, and were sometimes wounded, but they always won. Likewise, Superman fought the forces of evil in the name of "truth, justice, and the American way" and always won. *The Andy Griffith Show* pictured simple life in small-town America, projecting an idyllic picture of good and moral communities. These movies and television programs had a major, even if unrecognized, role in shaping my view of life and the world.

Like many kids at this age, I dabbled in collecting stamps and coins and assembling model cars. Eventually, playing chess became one of my main interests. The son of a Greek family that lived next to my grand-mother was also an avid chess player, and we played often. It was through him that I first encountered anti-Semitism. For some reason he disliked Jewish people and had audio recordings of some of Hitler's speeches. I listened to a few with him and found them transfixing, even though I didn't understand German. That seemingly minor experience planted a seed that would bear bitter fruit in the years ahead.

Around this time, into my emotional cauldron came a new feeling to join my anger and frustration: fear. Its origin lay in the events in the once-sleepy island nation of Cuba. For me, and for a lot of Americans, the 1960s were a decade defined by fear. When the Communists were making advances in faraway places like Southeast Asia and Eastern Europe, the threat did not seem quite so imminent. Suddenly, however, in 1959 Communists were in Cuba. Alarmed, Americans demanded action. But the 1961 CIA-sponsored Bay of Pigs invasion was a miserable failure. It was followed in short succession by failures in the Berlin crisis of 1961 and the Communist construction of the Berlin Wall.

These events embarrassed the United States. They signaled weakness. They revealed indecision in the White House and created uncertainty about America's leadership. People like me, who were concerned about the spread of totalitarian evil, were greatly discouraged. I wondered, *How could the greatest, most powerful nation on earth fail to dislodge the Communist dictator at our doorstep?*

Then came more unsettling news. The Soviet Union began the military reinforcement of the Castro regime. Even worse, American U-2 spy planes photographed Soviet nuclear missile launch facilities under construction at bases they had secretly built. The Cuban missile crisis generated unprecedented fear in the United States, especially in cities like Mobile that were now in range of a nuclear strike. With its large air force base and a busy shipping port, Mobile seemed an attractive target.

I remember watching TV news footage of U.S. warships confronting

Soviet ships in the Atlantic. Americans watched the dramatic confrontation play out on television, not knowing what might happen. The threat of nuclear war was ever present and very real.

As if Communism weren't enough of a threat to the nation, the nascent civil rights movement presented a rising threat to the national status quo. I became more aware of it when the Congress of Racial Equality sent Freedom Riders from Washington, DC, on a bus trip through the South. Violent opposition had erupted along the way, putting race relations squarely in the headlines and further escalating racial tensions. In the Mobile newspaper, I saw photographs and read about lunch-counter protests in Greensboro, North Carolina, and the burning of Freedom Rider buses.

Then came the enrollment of James Meredith in the University of Mississippi in October 1962. Mississippi governor Ross Barnett, another strong segregationist, publicly opposed desegregation, as did most white Mississippians. Deadly rioting broke out at Ole Miss, requiring U.S. marshals and federal troops to restore order. I read about the violence in the newspaper, but I was only fifteen at the time. Nothing like that was happening in Mobile, and the problems were too far away to make a big impression on me. But that event, along with the earlier race-related events challenging the status quo, was laying a foundation that would fuel my opposition to the civil rights movement.

In June 1963, Alabama governor George Wallace, in defiance of a federal court order, stood in the doorway of Foster Auditorium at the University of Alabama to block admission of two African American students. This high-drama media event was his way of fulfilling a promise from his inaugural speech a few months earlier: "In the name of the greatest people that have ever trod this earth, I draw the line in the dust and toss the gauntlet before the feet of tyranny . . . and I say . . . segregation now . . . segregation tomorrow . . . segregation forever."[1]

A dramatic confrontation ensued with United States deputy attorney general Nicholas Katzenbach and was nationally televised. Wallace was ordered to step aside. He refused. Mr. Katzenbach called President Kennedy, who immediately federalized the Alabama National Guard, which was standing with Wallace. The students were then admitted.[2]

Most white people in Alabama, however, were strongly supportive of Governor Wallace. Like many others, I was outraged by the incident. I was incensed at the federal government for intruding in what I believed to be state affairs. A few weeks later, Governor Wallace denounced the civil rights movement as part of the Communist conspiracy. Not long afterward, I read an article alleging that the FBI had discovered that certain civil rights leaders were associating with known Communists. I believed these things were true, and I was alarmed.

On June 12, the day after Wallace's stand in the schoolhouse door, Medgar Evers, a field secretary for the National Association for the Advancement of Colored People (NAACP), was murdered in Jackson, Mississippi. He had been working tirelessly to overturn segregation and secure better opportunities for African Americans in Mississippi.

Shortly afterward, the U.S. Supreme Court handed down a ruling banning prayer and Bible reading in public schools. I was shocked. When I was in grade school, my teachers briefly read the Bible to us and prayed at the start of each day. What was wrong with that? Why abolish it? I felt that something was seriously wrong in America. To me, it was clear that the government was now undermining the very principles on which America had been built.

A month later, civil rights leaders brought together a quarter of a million people from around the country to protest for civil rights in the nation's capital. Here, Dr. Martin Luther King Jr. gave his famous "I Have a Dream" speech at the Lincoln Memorial.

These events were part of a major social upheaval in the South and elsewhere in America. What had been considered normal for decades in our part of the country was now being challenged and attacked by the federal government: segregation was being abolished, states' rights were being trampled on, and Christianity was being repudiated. How could this be happening? It felt as though the established order of society was being overturned—and by our own government. These rapid social changes were very disorienting for me and many others. And they fed fear and anger.

*     *     *

In the summer of 1963, my dad received some material in the mail from the Draft Goldwater Committee. I read it and got involved in getting signatures on petitions that were enclosed in the letter. Goldwater's book *The Conscience of a Conservative* showed that he was patriotic and looked like a good alternative to Kennedy. He seemed to be a strong leader who would fight Communist aggression, rein in government overreach, and hopefully halt desegregation. The people I met during this brief period were good, upstanding citizens and conservative in political orientation but not extremists. I wish I had stopped there.

But after pursuing this for a number of weeks, I stumbled on some literature from the John Birch Society, which exposed me to additional troubling concerns and took me to a different level. I had never heard of the organization, but they had members in Mobile. After talking with some of them and reading their literature, I concluded that they were patriotic Americans. The Birchers were very concerned about the spread of world Communism and its growing influence in America, including its influence on the civil rights movement, which they opposed.

As I read more John Birch literature and then books such as *Masters of Deceit* by J. Edgar Hoover, I became increasingly alarmed about the spread of Communism around the world and in the United States. According to Hoover, Communist infiltration of the U.S. government and subversive activities in America were a real danger. If the director of the FBI saw Communism as such a serious threat to America, that settled it for me.

The John Birch Society was also concerned about the United Nations gaining control over the nations of the world and establishing a one-world government. Much of this coincided with what I had seen unfolding over the past several years, and I found it very disturbing. I now viewed the United Nations as a sinister threat to our national sovereignty. If the Birchers were correct, the United States was in danger of an imminent Communist takeover. I came to believe the nation was like a large and beautiful edifice that was being eaten away from within by termites. America could collapse at any time.

The impact of this viewpoint radically changed my outlook on life. As I saw it, the world was gradually being swallowed up by international Communism—Russia in 1917, Eastern Europe in 1945–46, China in 1947, Indochina in 1954, and Cuba in 1959. Tens of millions of people had been killed in the process. And the only nation strong enough to resist its spread was itself being undermined from within.

Communists had even infiltrated the U.S. government. Alger Hiss and others at the U.S. State Department were cited as examples. Klaus Fuchs, Julius and Ethel Rosenberg, and other spies in our nuclear program had given atomic secrets to the Soviets. Other Communist spies were still at work in the government and in the civil rights movement. Worst of all, most Americans seemed either unaware or unconcerned. To me, the situation seemed far too serious to be solved by electing Barry Goldwater. My interest in him evaporated, and I moved into the Birchers' orbit.

Looking back, I realize that I did not grasp the complexities of issues. I saw everything in terms of stark extremes, failing to consider possible areas of gray, and I gravitated toward simple answers to complicated questions. I had come to believe that the West was in the midst of an epic life-or-death struggle with worldwide Communism, which had penetrated America and was gaining ground. While such a struggle was real, I believed things were far worse than they actually were. This aroused fear in me and resulted in my emotions dominating my reason as I grappled with these concerns. It also intensified my patriotism.

As a high school student, I had not yet developed skills in critical thinking. I didn't investigate and reason through these issues very well. Nor did I seek the insights of older, wiser people with more experience in life. I accepted the pronouncements of charismatic or noteworthy personalities. My dad's idea of working through normal political and legal processes to address these problems made no sense to me. Based on what I was reading and hearing, I regarded such methods as futile and hopeless, because those in power either didn't understand the dangers or were afraid to act. All this propelled me toward extremism. I thought of myself as part of a small minority who could see the impending social and political disaster. I had a duty to warn the masses and to be engaged in the struggle. Psychologically, this sense of mission gave me a purpose and significance that I had never had.

I was coming to believe that this imminent threat to our nation had to be countered with direct action before it was too late. Somebody had to do something. The fear and anger I developed toward the perceived enemies of America began to feed a new emotion: hatred. At the age of seventeen, I was unwittingly leaving true patriotism behind and moving into the dark world of far-right extremism. And though supposedly a Christian, I was also leaving behind the moral values I had been taught and giving myself over to an increasingly self-indulgent, amoral lifestyle, which I still deeply regret.

About this time, one of the Birchers told me of a mysterious figure living in our area who was involved in anti-Castro guerrilla activities. The failed Bay of Pigs invasion of Cuba a couple of years earlier left some Cuban exiles wanting to continue covert military action. During those days numerous anti-Castro groups were engaged in guerrilla warfare and commando raids on Cuba. A staunch anti-Communist, this man had been on raids to Cuba himself. He was active in securing support and supplies for such groups in Florida.

Although my contact with him was brief, the exposure introduced me to the exciting but shadowy world of clandestine activities and international intrigue. I assumed these efforts were sanctioned and covertly supported by the Central Intelligence Agency (CIA), and because it was anti-Communist, I saw it as a heroic and patriotic effort to fight Communist aggression.

This experience intensified my interest in guerrilla warfare, counterinsurgency, sabotage, intelligence work, and clandestine operations. I read many books from the public library on these subjects during the months and years that followed, becoming well versed in these areas. I also developed a great interest in firearms and marksmanship. I studied in such detail that I could identify and operate a number of the nation's military small arms and cite their specifications.

My parents were unaware of how rapidly my thinking was evolving and the direction it was taking me. As I raised some of my concerns with my father, he tried to allay them by giving me historical perspective. He thought the social and political changes under way would run for a number of years, then swing back to a more normal point. But that long-range view didn't register with me.

By the end of the summer of 1963, I was becoming increasingly radical. I had made significant progress in preparing myself to help protect America from the evils that were threatening to destroy her. I merely needed some practical experience. The desegregation of Murphy High School in Mobile provided the first opportunity.

# DESCENDING INTO DARKNESS

The racial integration of Alabama's public schools began in September 1963, while I was a high school student. Earlier in the year, two federal court rulings targeted Mobile's public schools for integration. Segregationist organizations called for rallies and organized conferences in an effort to mobilize people and plan resistance. As the opening day of school drew nearer, tensions mounted throughout the state of Alabama but were particularly strong in Mobile.

Again and again, I heard responsible people charging that states' rights were being violated, the Constitution was being undermined, one-world government was on the horizon, Communists controlled the civil rights movement, desegregation would result in interracial marriage, and all of this would lead to the fall of "white Christian civilization." My parents had not raised me to be a racist, but this kind of inflammatory rhetoric helped me become one.

When school began on September 4, 1963, I seemed like many other seventeen-year-olds. I had a driver's license and a desire to get out and about town and have fun. But inside I was also an angry, frustrated teenager. In addition to my troubled home life and my unrecognized inner conflicts and tensions, I was furious at the idea of the federal government forcing my state and high school to integrate—especially in view of the alleged Communist influence in the civil rights movement. The arrogance of it was staggering. The impact was now personal. My already huge payload of anger and frustration was exceeded only by my sense of personal grievance.

The U.S. government seemed to be going right along with what the Communists wanted—just like what I was being taught about the growing Communist menace in America. My radical influences were being proven correct. Southern values—indeed the whole Southern way of life—were under attack. My inner turmoil at this disorienting social upheaval would eventually produce tragic consequences. To my anti-Communism, I had added a strong dislike for the federal government for trampling states' rights and forcing integration. I was about to add hatred for black people for desegregating my school and Southern society in general.

I arrived on the huge campus of Murphy High School about half an hour before the two black girls were to arrive for registration. Already on the campus were dozens of U.S. marshals, Alabama state troopers, and Mobile city police, all backed by armed National Guard troops in jeeps. I was outraged at what looked and felt like the armed occupation of my high school. The show of force—especially military force—was intimidating. It felt as if the government was against the people. Surely, they expected trouble and were taking no chances.

I talked with other students to see what resistance was planned. No one knew of any. I was shocked. I tried to encourage friends and groups of students to make a protest of some sort, but my efforts were in vain. *What a spineless bunch*, I thought in disgust. Later that morning, however, a group of students did demonstrate in protest, and a small riot ensued, but I had already left and had no part in it.

I was so incensed by the situation that I telephoned Governor George Wallace's office in Montgomery and asked to speak to him directly. Though I didn't get through to him, I respectfully warned his office that tension was high and trouble was likely if he didn't take action to block the desegregation.

The principal at my school was told of my call by state officials. He labeled me a troublemaker and suspended me for several days. My first day back in school, I began harassing the two black girls, and I encouraged others to do the same. I called them all sorts of hateful, derogatory names. I even hit and shoved them when I thought I could get away with it. Had they been boys, I probably would have tried to beat them up.

On November 22, 1963, the school's public address system interrupted classes to broadcast throughout the school that President Kennedy had been shot in Dallas, Texas. I was sitting in my Latin class at the time and remember it well. Early reports were unclear, but soon came the announcement that the president had been killed. Although the news was shocking, like so many others in the South, I was not sorry to hear it. Kennedy's strong anti-Communist position had been eclipsed by his support for the civil rights movement. That poisoned his image for many Southerners.

*       *       *

Around that time, someone gave me a copy of the *Thunderbolt*, a newspaper published by the National States Rights Party (NSRP), which contained articles purporting to show that black people were intellectually inferior to whites, that white women were in danger of being raped by black men, that race mixing resulted in cultural decline, and that the Communist threat and the civil rights movement were both Jewish in origin. This seemed plausible to me, so I sought further understanding from the NSRP, a far-right organization that was active in protesting the desegregation. I first met the leader of the Mobile chapter at the local NSRP office. He helped me see that it was a waste of time to make Murphy High School a priority in the fight against integration and Communism. There were bigger battles to be fought, battles that would have a much greater impact. Soon after meeting him, I became active in the local NSRP, though my involvement would be short-lived.

I discovered that the NSRP was essentially a neo-Nazi group with beliefs almost identical to the various Ku Klux Klan groups. Founded in 1958, they were a much smaller organization than the Birchers, who were not neo-Nazi. Moreover, they were a different type of people. For the most part, the Birchers I had met were educated professionals, established in the community, and opposed to anti-Semitism and to violence. The NSRP was just the opposite—not well educated, very anti-Semitic, and publicly opposed to violence but secretly open to it.

I often went to the local office to learn more about how the Jews were behind both global Communism and the U.S. civil rights movement. As I continued to read the *Thunderbolt*, it reinforced what I had been hearing. Its book reviews, articles, and advertisements repeated the message of anti-Semitism and neo-Nazism. One of the books I bought was *The Protocols of the Learned Elders of Zion*, purportedly the minutes of meetings by Jewish leaders outlining their plans for world domination. It painted a picture of a secret, powerful conspiracy that aimed to influence the press, the economy, the political system, and much more to gain increasing control over the Gentile world. This gave me the framework for a conspiratorial view of world affairs that was filled in later by other anti-Semitic literature, all of which aroused fear and anger.

Adolf Hitler said, "The most brilliant propagandist technique will yield no success unless one fundamental principle is borne in mind constantly—it must confine itself to a few points and repeat them over and over."[1] There is truth in this idea, which psychologists call the "illusion of truth" effect.[2] This phenomenon explains what was happening to me at age seventeen, as I was filling my head with a few extreme ideas, repeated again and again in different ways.

Anti-Semitism was not a natural progression for me. Just the opposite, in fact. I had known a couple of Jewish girls in grade school and liked them both, and they liked me. My grandmother had worked for a jewelry store owned by a respected Jewish family in Mobile. They had treated her well, and she always had good things to say about them. Although I had picked up a slight negative attitude toward Jews from my Greek friend who had exposed me to the Hitler recordings, I had no animosity toward them. But what I was now hearing and reading was changing my attitude toward Jews dramatically.

I spent even more time with another NSRP member, an older guy who was a good friend of the organization's leader. He met me at least once a week, sometimes more. Since I was not involved in any sports or after-school activities, it fit right in with my social schedule. When school let out in the afternoons, he would take me to a coffee shop, or we would go to his house. Sometimes we would just drive around and talk. We listened repeatedly to the recorded sermons and lectures of Dr. Wesley Swift, an anti-Semitic and racist former Methodist minister from California who preached white supremacy. His sermons influenced my beliefs and attitudes toward Jewish people more than anything else. Swift's racist theology, called Christian Identity, would eventually give rise to the violent and dangerous Aryan Nations movement, which is still active today.

Swift claimed that he taught the true Christian religion. Starting with ideas of a little-known sect called British Israelism, which contends that white northern Europeans are actually descendants of the ten lost tribes of Israel, he created an anti-Semitic, racist theology. Swift preached that those who are now called Jews are not true Israelites but are descended from the ungodly line of Cain. (Cain, the first son of Adam and Eve, was said by Swift to be the offspring of the Devil, who seduced Eve.) True Israelites are those who are descended from the godly line of Seth, the third son of Adam. Most of them were deported to Assyria when Israel's ten northern tribes were taken captive in 722 BC. These tribes later migrated to northern Europe and are the ancestors of the Anglo-Saxon peoples found in Europe (and now in America and elsewhere). It is from this bloodline that Jesus was supposedly descended.

According to Swift, the pseudo-Jews of today are an evil, anti-Christian race, and key leaders among them have long been secretly conspiring to gain control of the world through Communism and race mixing, both of which they used as tools. Black people, Swift taught, were subhuman, had no souls, and were being used by the Jews to intermarry with whites, to generate a mongrel race that would be more easily controlled. In the last days, the evil line of Cain and the godly line of Seth would engage in mortal combat. With God's help, the line of Seth would prevail. It was therefore important for all those of the line of Seth (white European stock) to prepare themselves by obtaining weapons and munitions of various sorts and learning to use them as they await the coming battle.

Not knowing the Bible very well, I overlaid the little understanding I did have with this dangerous religious ideology, not realizing the errors I was embracing. Swift's ideology appealed to me because it reinforced my prejudices and gave them a religious justification.

Through reading books and papers, attending meetings, listening to recordings, and talking with others, my beliefs became ever more extreme, fueling anger toward perceived enemies of America and white Christian civilization. In my mind, America's enemies were evil, and it did not take long for my anger to grow into hatred, not just for specific individuals but for entire groups and races—Communists, Jews, and blacks. This stereotyping and demonizing made it possible to indiscriminately hate the "enemy." The combination of extreme political beliefs undergirded by a religious justification created the sense of a "holy cause." God was on our side. Therefore, he could not possibly be on the other side. Any means necessary were justified to achieve God's purposes. If it cost our lives, that would not be loss but gain, since we would go on to God's reward for our heroic service.

I had become what American philosopher Eric Hoffer called a "true believer."[3] Ironically, the intensity of my commitment is captured in the words of a young Communist:

> There is one thing about which I am completely in earnest—the Communist cause. It is my life, my business, my religion, my hobby, my sweetheart, my wife, my mistress, my meat and drink. I work at it by day and dream of it by night. Its control over me grows greater with the passage of time. Therefore I cannot have a friend, a lover or even a conversation without relating them to this power that animates and controls my life. I measure people, books, ideas and deeds according to the way they affect the Communist cause and by their attitude to it. I have already been in jail for my ideas, and if need be, I am ready to face death.[4]

This man's all-consuming dedication to Communism, which I hated, mirrored my own all-consuming devotion to the Far Right. I had begun with a kind of grassroots conservatism, then left it behind as I moved steadily toward the farthest point to the right on the political spectrum. That point was a small, racist, neo-Nazi world, rejected by classic conservatives, who called it "the lunatic fringe." We, in turn, rejected them as blind or as compromisers. My intense sense of grievance had led to a major change in my worldview, and I had become radicalized.

The far-right world I now occupied was far removed from the political conservatism I encountered when I first took an interest in politics. People were more open to use violence to achieve their goals. Perhaps their most prominent ideological distinctive was a vicious anti-Semitism. The Far Right held that Communism and most of the other ills affecting society were products of an international conspiracy among certain powerful and wealthy Jews, usually international Jewish bankers, such as the Rothschilds. Everything was interpreted through this filter: Communism was a Jewish plot to take over the world; America's social problems were Jewish-inspired schemes to weaken society; racial integration was a Jewish scheme to destroy the white race through intermarriage with nonwhites. A Communist-Jewish takeover was just ahead, and we needed to get prepared and fight it.

As I absorbed more and more of this thinking, I developed a deepening hatred that consumed me. I hated blacks, but I loathed the Jews, who were the supposed masterminds of the civil rights movement. In school I began picking on some of the Jewish students. At first, I used racial slurs, calling them "kikes" and "Jewish dogs" in the presence of their friends. Then I began to threaten them with violence. On one occasion, I picked on a Jewish student, and he reacted with a hostile remark. Although he had never done anything to me, I roughed him up pretty bad on the spot, and I threatened to kill him. Apparently, he didn't tell anyone, because I didn't get in any trouble for it. I eventually began punching some of the guys when I had the chance. One Jewish boy, whose family owned a local jewelry store, was about my age and took the brunt of my anger. He was a mild-mannered young man and never fought back. He had never done anything to me. But my anti-Semitic hatred had blinded me to common decency and respect for anyone Jewish. I even engaged in verbal harassment and insults toward Jewish girls.

Bad ideas have bad consequences. My transition from normal thinking to ideological thinking was surprisingly quick, a result at least in part of my poorly developed critical thinking skills. In addition, I had a limited base of knowledge with which to evaluate what I was hearing (which is key to overcoming the "illusion of truth" effect of propaganda). I also had little, if any, willingness to talk with my family or utilize other rational influences to help me process these twisted beliefs. Rather, I only listened to voices reinforcing them. I soon became impervious to anything or anyone outside of my ideological bubble. And this ideology, with its strong call to patriotism, became all the more potent by the addition of a religious dimension, giving it divine sanction and removing any fear of death. The potentially disastrous consequences of this way of thinking was not evident to me. I was looking in another direction. My fight would be the noblest of all: the Cause of God and country, which my newfound friends were urging.

*       *       *

From September 1963 through early 1964, while keeping my parents in the dark, I studied these themes intensely and met regularly with local "patriots," as they called themselves. Through these meetings, I gradually made contact with other extremists in the area.

One night at the local headquarters, the leader of the Mobile chapter of the NSRP introduced me to two highly committed radicals. They were friends of his who had recently moved to Mobile from Miami. One had been a pilot, and the other had been in business. They were part of a group in Miami that, under pressure from law enforcement, had left to form an underground network in the Southeast. The actual specifics of their problems with the law in Miami were never mentioned. I knew better than to ask, so I never learned. These two were cautious, so our relationship developed more slowly than with others I knew from the NSRP. They met with me numerous times to discuss ideology and to gain a sense of how committed I was. Over the course of several months they came to trust me.

I also came to know a couple in their sixties from the Miami area who were among the extremists who had relocated to the Mobile area. I spent many hours in their home, discussing the "Communist-Jewish conspiracy" and listening to Wesley Swift tapes. In some ways this couple was an enigma. The husband was suspicious to the point of being paranoid. He talked a lot about hating the Jews but was never inclined to take action.

From these ex-Miami radicals and the way they operated, I learned the practical aspects of conducting clandestine activities. Everything was done in strict security. We would meet at prearranged rendezvous points, observing painstaking procedures to assure that we were not followed. Because of possible bugging, important matters were discussed only in secure places, hardly ever in our homes, offices, or automobiles. To circumvent FBI wire taps, we never discussed anything on the phone. Meeting places and people were referred to in veiled terms or by use of code words.

The many hours we spent together discussing ideology, strategy, and tactics deepened our relationships and trained me as an extremist. I felt an increased need to give myself to this vital cause. The more conversant I became with these ideas and doctrines, the more outspoken I was on the need for action, the more approval and recognition I gained. Indeed, I became quite articulate. The more skillful I was in planning and implementing ideas for action, small though they were at this point, the faster I gained the confidence of these men.

Barely eighteen, I was becoming a trusted member of the radical group in Mobile. While my parents knew that my thinking had become more extreme, they had no idea I was associating with real extremists.

By February 1964, I was obsessed with my new ideology. Disinterested in high school, lacking sufficient credits to graduate with my class, and eager for more direct action, I dropped out and went to Montgomery to meet with Admiral John G. Crommelin, a prominent anti-Semite and frequent candidate for public office. Admiral Crommelin was a good friend of my colleagues and was regarded as a great patriot. I had met him briefly when he was in Mobile a few months earlier making a televised political speech, and I was duly impressed. It was exciting to meet someone like him. A man of his stature was an iconic figure to the Cause and gave it credibility in my mind.

Admiral Crommelin was a graduate of the U.S. Naval Academy and a decorated hero from World War II. He had served as executive officer of the aircraft carrier USS *Enterprise*, the most decorated ship of the war. A gruff old man in his sixties, the admiral lived in retirement in Montgomery, where he had a comfortable home as well as a large country estate.

I arrived in Montgomery on a cold, gray winter day. The admiral's wife, Lillian, was waiting at the bus station. She drove me out to their country home, named Harrogate Springs. The admiral was in conference with several men about political issues, but he took a moment to cordially greet me and show me to a guest room; then he returned to his visitors. Later that evening, and for several days, we talked at length about the "Communist-Jewish conspiracy." He was highly knowledgeable and outspoken about his beliefs, a trait that had gotten him into trouble in the navy. Why he took time to talk with me is a mystery, but his beliefs and strength of conviction conferred credibility. Admiral Crommelin made a powerful impression on me and reinforced my own convictions as he repeated what I had heard and read a number of times already about the Communist-Jewish conspiracy.

From Montgomery I traveled on to NSRP national headquarters in Birmingham to meet with Dr. Edward Fields, the executive director. However, it was not a particularly warm meeting, and I later learned that he regarded me as a loose cannon who might damage the NSRP's work. After a brief visit, I returned to Mobile and gave myself more passionately to the work of the Cause.

*     *     *

From my point of view, the racial situation in the South seemed to be worsening. Freedom Summer began in June of that year, 1964, with more than a thousand people coming to Mississippi to help black people register to vote. This evoked widespread resentment among whites, who felt the state was being invaded by Northern liberals determined to impose their views on them. Tensions were rising dramatically.

The White Knights of the Ku Klux Klan met this challenge first with threats and then with violence. A group of Klansmen abducted and murdered three young civil rights workers—James Earl Chaney, Andrew Goodman, and Michael Schwerner. This led to a nationwide outcry and a massive search by federal, state, and local authorities. The discovery of their bodies gave momentum to stalled efforts in Congress to pass the Civil Rights Act of 1964, in July. A few months later, eighteen members of the White Knights of the KKK, including Imperial Wizard Sam Bowers, were arrested and charged with conspiracy to deprive the three of their civil rights, which was a serious offense. Now the government would enforce more desegregation measures that would lead to race mixing and interracial marriage. In my mind, the country was continuing to spiral downward.

The American South was in upheaval. Our values were being challenged in areas of race, sex, drugs, and more. The traditions we had known and accepted for decades were being destroyed before my eyes. What previously had seemed to be nailed down and stable was being torn from its moorings by Communist-leaning liberals and Jews from the North. As I saw it, the world I lived in was full of turmoil, and the norms of society were collapsing. And only a few people seemed to be doing anything to stop it.

The KKK's willingness to take action appealed to me. They were a group I wanted to make contact with at some point.

Meanwhile, another major issue was emerging in the United States: the Vietnam War was escalating. There was great concern about the spread of Communism in Southeast Asia and fear of a domino effect if South Vietnam fell. I remember the graphic front-page photos in the Mobile newspaper of the bullet-riddled body of South Vietnam President Diem, who was assassinated in late 1963. The Communist threat in Asia got my attention and temporarily distracted me from threats in the United States. In 1964 I went to the U.S. Army recruiting office in Mobile to explore enlistment, with a preference for Ranger School.

It would have been the wisest possible decision for me.

But at the last minute I decided against it. My disgust for President Lyndon Johnson was so intense that I could not put myself under his authority as commander in chief. Instead of going to battle abroad, I decided to continue my present course and redouble my efforts to fight the Communist-Jewish conspiracy at home.

# OPENING SKIRMISHES

B y the fall of 1964, I was convinced that my country was in great
danger, but most people were asleep. As a patriotic American, I was
deeply frustrated by this. Something had to be done. I couldn't do everything, but I could do something, and what I could do, I should do—even
if it landed me in jail.

My campaign against the "enemies of America" began with relatively
minor acts of political harassment. Initially, this took the form of threatening phone calls to the rabbis of Mobile's two synagogues and to the
local head of the Jewish Anti-Defamation League. I had heard that the
police could not trace phone calls if they lasted only a few seconds, so I
made the calls from my grandmother's house, unbeknownst to her. The
messages were very short. I was nervous making the first call. "We know
who you are, what you are up to, and how to find you," was the essence
of the message. Then the calls got easier. I called black civil rights leaders
in the area as well, with the same message. Whether others were doing

things like this, I didn't know or care. I had at least done something. I had struck a blow against the enemy, however small. But my satisfaction from this activity was short-lived. Ultimately, it turned out to be just a cheap thrill. I wanted concrete action, not just words.

My grandmother and my parents would have been horrified to know what I had done. I did not hide my increasingly radical beliefs, but I was careful to conceal my activities and the people with whom I was associating.

I settled for continued harassment, but of a more concrete sort. Late one night, I nervously walked on back streets the few blocks to the synagogue near my grandmother's house, where I was spending the weekend. After making certain that there was no one was around, I pulled out a can of red spray paint concealed under my shirt and painted a couple of swastikas on the back of the building. This caused a furor among the Jewish community. The police investigated but had no evidence or leads to follow, and nothing came of it. In the weeks that followed, I also made several calls to the synagogue during their services, threatening violence.

Far from satisfying my hostility, this behavior only intensified it. Words might satisfy some, but for me they stirred up a desire for action. Some of my close friends and I began actively discussing even stronger acts of intimidation.

The next step in the escalating pattern of violence was firing shots into the houses of those we had identified as enemies. During my first few months of nonviolent fighting for the Cause, I had purchased various legal firearms, which were readily available in gun shops to anyone with the money to pay. Illegal weapons, like submachine guns, were also available if one knew where to go and had the money. I also diligently practiced marksmanship, which was strongly encouraged as preparation for the coming Communist-Jewish takeover. So far I had been able to keep my parents in the dark about what I was doing. And because guns were such a common part of Southern culture, I suppose my parents didn't think it was particularly unusual for me to buy a few.

A fellow radical and I began by shooting into the houses of black civil rights leaders late at night to create fear and stir up unrest. Usually one of us would drive and the other would do the shooting. We struck when few people would be out to identify our car—but not so late that we would be conspicuous. On many occasions we struck while the police were changing shifts, sometimes using radios to monitor police calls. For months, we waged a campaign of terror against the black community. On one occasion, we even fired into the white mayor's house, who in our opinion was soft on race mixing.

Although part of our strategy included creating fear and terror in the black community, it was more important to produce racial polarization and retaliation. If our actions provoked a few of the more radical blacks in town to attack whites, we believed this would then swell the ranks of whites who would be willing to condone or employ violence as a viable response to the racial problem. From our perspective, this was a highly desirable, totally justified course of action, even though it might result in some white casualties. We feared that as long as peaceful race relations prevailed—and they generally did in Mobile—integration could proceed unhindered and eventually bring about interracial marriage. We got these ideas from an older radical who seemed to be very committed to the Cause and frequently came up with ideas for violence. It later became obvious that he was an agent provocateur.

If the polarization and retaliation had occurred as we hoped, we planned to kill selected Jewish, white, and black leaders during the ensuing confusion. We also had a mobilization plan for responding to attack. If one of our friends or sympathizers was attacked by a black, or if a confrontation developed, he could call a central number distributed on a printed business card. From the central number, calls would go out to about a dozen people, each of whom would alert another dozen, and so on. Heavily armed, each would respond to the alert by proceeding to the scene for appropriate action. This network plan was called the Christian Military Defense League ("Christian" because we all considered ourselves Christians). However, with fewer than a dozen people who expressed interest, it went nowhere.

I didn't realize what was happening to me as I was descending into this abyss of hatred and violence. As C. S. Lewis observed, "Every time you make a choice you are turning the central part of you, the part of you that chooses, into something a little different from what it was before. And taking your life as a whole, with all your innumerable choices, all your life long you are slowly turning this central thing into a heavenly creature or into a hellish creature."[1] My choices were turning me into a hellish creature.

In August 1964, after almost a year in the radical movement in Mobile, I got into serious trouble for the first time. Late one night I was driving through the black section of town with the local NSRP leader. I don't remember why we were there, but the police saw us and pulled us over for a routine search. They found a .38-caliber revolver and my sawed-off shotgun. I was arrested and charged with violation of the Federal Firearms Act. This was a serious offense.

Before this, I had been questioned several times by the Mobile Police Department about violence in the area. The detective who questioned me on these occasions was a friend of my dad's. He tried to warn me about what I was getting myself into. But I shrugged it off. Now his prediction had come true.

From the time of my arrest until the sentencing in May 1966, a period of almost two years, I was more active than ever—but also much more cautious. Through the efforts of my attorney and the mercy of the U.S. district court judge, I was placed on probation until my twenty-first birthday. The judge said, "If I ever hear of you associating with another radical or touching another gun—even a shotgun for dove hunting—I will revoke your probation and send you to prison." After the sentencing, I had no choice but to discontinue most of my activities and meet less frequently with my friends.

During this period, I read about another murder in Mississippi. Vernon Dahmer, president of the Hattiesburg, Mississippi, NAACP chapter, had been killed. His home was firebombed and riddled with gunfire by a large group of men. Dahmer returned fire and fought back, allowing his wife and children to escape, but he was seriously burned and died the next day. Fourteen Klansmen were indicted. In spite of the arrests in the Philadelphia, Mississippi case a couple of years earlier, this showed that the White Knights of the Ku Klux Klan were still active. This attracted my attention and increased my interest in making contact with them.

Early in the summer of 1967, I noticed that the FBI and police no longer watched me as closely as they had been. By now my thinking had matured some—at least to the extent of thinking more strategically rather than just tactically. Two things seemed clear to me. First, the part of the Far Right I knew about could never hope to achieve its goals without high-level unity. That was practically nonexistent as far as I could tell. Second, rank-and-file radicals around the country needed to have a common identity. I was now almost twenty-one and considered myself an effective freedom fighter. I also knew some of the top leaders of the movement and had access to others. By developing my relationships with these leaders while at the same time conducting a major anti-Jewish terrorist operation, I thought I could promote unity. In any case, I would be advancing my position and power within the movement. It never occurred to me that it would take years for someone as young as I was to accomplish such a thing, if, indeed, it could be accomplished at all.

Sooner or later, in every battle, lines are drawn. Mississippi had become the front line in the battle against the civil rights movement. And it was on the front lines that I belonged.

# 7

# INTO THE THICK OF BATTLE

F ully immersed in conspiracy theories and ideology, and convinced
that I knew the truth, I was now ready to make contacts among Ku
Klux Klan leaders, starting in Alabama and moving out from there. I contacted Robert Shelton, imperial wizard of the United Klans of America,
the largest of the various independent Klan organizations around the
country and headquartered in Alabama. Because I had the recommendation of a longtime Klan leader in south Alabama, it was a relatively simple
matter to arrange a meeting. I was hoping to establish a good relationship
that might lead to other things in the future.

I drove to Tuscaloosa to meet with Shelton. After coffee at a downtown restaurant, we drove to his lakeside home, where he lived with his
family. There, we conducted Klan business for about an hour, exchanging
thoughts on a variety of issues related to the Communist-Jewish conspiracy. Then I returned to Mobile, promising to keep in touch. I felt good

about the rapport that our time had established and was confident that our relationship would mature in the days to come (though it never did because I became involved with the Mississippi Klan instead).

A couple of months later, I drove to Laurel, Mississippi, to meet with Klan leader Sam Bowers. At that time, the Mississippi Klan was the most violent right-wing terrorist organization in America, according to the FBI. Bowers was the logical person to approach. Because Mississippi authorities had so many local suspects to investigate, I reasoned it would be a good place for an out-of-stater to operate without detection. I found Bowers to be articulate and intelligent, with a phenomenal memory and a mind for detail. Though initially suspicious, Bowers accepted me once I had proven my trustworthiness. We became close associates, even though I never officially joined the Mississippi Klan.

Sam Bowers was largely a closed person, and few knew him intimately. He and I had a working relationship based on common ideology and goals, but we never developed what you would call a real friendship. Strange as it may seem, Bowers was a religious man, as were many Klansmen in those days—religious in the sense that he believed God existed and occasionally attended church. However, the only time we ever talked about religion, I did most of the talking. It never was entirely clear to me just exactly what his specific religious beliefs were. I assumed they were the common views of most Southern racists in those days—a version of fundamentalism that held that black people were descendants of Noah's son Ham, and were dark-skinned, less intelligent, and backward because they had been placed under a curse, and that the Bible forbade the mixing of the races.

Bowers was often under surveillance by the FBI, so we had to meet under the most careful of security procedures. We nearly always met at prearranged rendezvous points at night—usually in remote wooded areas. To assure that our meeting places were safe, we changed them each time. We feared the FBI's sophisticated electronic monitoring equipment.

Even in clandestine meeting places, our conversations were extremely guarded. Often, we would leave our cars and walk somewhere so our conversations could not be detected by electronic bugs. On one occasion, we met at his office to discuss some important matters. Instead of talking, we sat at a table and wrote out our thoughts on notebook paper and exchanged them. When we finished, he burned the papers, ground the ashes, placed them in a bucket of water, and then flushed them down the toilet in his washroom.

The FBI's Counterintelligence Program, though unknown to us at the time, was quite effective. Our great fear of FBI undercover agents, phone taps, and listening devices produced a near epidemic of paranoia in the Klan. We were suspicious of nearly everyone. There were many ideas for acts of violence and many people who would have carried them out. But everyone was reluctant to develop and implement them due to the ever-present possibility of being overheard by FBI devices or betrayed by an undercover agent or informer, of which there were many. This was part of the bureau's strategy. And it was quite effective. Had it not been for this fear of the FBI and its infiltration, and the internal paranoia and distrust it generated, I believe there would have been a much higher level of violence in the sixties than actually occurred.

Because of the FBI's effectiveness in paralyzing Klan operations through fear and distrust, and because of the convictions in the highly publicized Philadelphia case and Dahmer case, the Klan was now reeling. The enemy had gained the upper hand, and the future looked dismal.

In the fall of 1967, the Klan's resistance shifted in a different direction. In addition to targeting African Americans and white civil rights activists, it expanded its terror campaign to Mississippi's Jewish population as well. A string of bombings in rapid succession against Jews along with these other groups created a climate of fear.

The Klan's terror campaign was succeeding beyond its hopes. After five bombs in two months, terror was rampant among Mississippi's Jewish and black communities. The national news media were focused on Mississippi. Frustrated and paralyzed Klansmen around the state were encouraged by these acts of violence, and so was I. *Maybe the Klan could make a comeback*, I hoped.

But these acts drew intense attention from national law enforcement. FBI director J. Edgar Hoover ordered additional FBI agents into the state to assist the widening investigations. These agents would form the lead elements of a massive, coordinated interagency effort dedicated to halting the Klan's reign of terror. No effort would be spared to bring the new outbreak of terror to a halt and the guilty to justice.

*       *       *

On December 20, 1967, on a cold, rainy afternoon in Laurel, I met with Sam Bowers for one of our periodic strategy sessions. That night we drove west on Highway 84 about twenty miles to Collins, Mississippi. We intended to machine-gun the home of a local black man who had fired on a police officer some days earlier. However, we couldn't find his house. After driving around the darkened town, we pulled into a closed service station to recheck our directions. A local police car pulled in behind us.

The officer approached my car with a big flashlight and asked for my driver's license. After inspecting it under his beam, he commented on my Alabama license plates. He asked why I was in that little town on a rainy December night. Various thoughts were racing through my mind as I tried to assess our options in a split second and decide what to do. *Can I talk my way out of this? What if he decides to call for help or take us in for questioning? Should we take him captive, handcuff him to a nearby lamppost, and make a fast getaway?* I could not quickly come up with a convincing answer. He shone the light over to Sam and asked if he had identification. Sam pulled out his wallet and presented his driver's license.

The officer's eyes registered his recognition of Sam Bowers's name. He decided to take us down to the station "just to ask a few questions," then returned to his car and radioed for backup. We stayed put.

At the Covington County Jail, the officer conducted a "routine search" of my car and found my loaded .45-caliber submachine gun under a sweater on the front seat. The policemen on duty became very excited. The desk clerk started dialing the telephone and covered the mouthpiece when he talked. The FBI and Mississippi state police immediately answered those calls. We were arrested and placed in a holding cell.

This was bad—really bad. My cover was blown. Bowers and I had now been publicly linked. Soon the federal government would be seeking an indictment against me for possession of a submachine gun, a federal offense. Ironically, I had just turned twenty-one, so my previous illegal gun charge could not be held against me.

I was really worried. Sam and I were preparing to commit a federal crime when we had been caught red-handed with all the evidence necessary to prove intent and conspiracy to commit that crime.

The FBI ran a check on the serial number of my car and discovered it had been stolen several months before I bought it—one of the many cars "dumped" in Mississippi before title registration was required. This could potentially lead to a charge of possession of stolen property.

Somehow, despite the ongoing high-profile reign of terror in the state and being caught with an illegal, fully loaded submachine gun, Imperial Wizard Sam Bowers of the Mississippi Ku Klux Klan and I were released on bond the next day. I decided this might be a good time to leave Mississippi before my luck ran out altogether.

In a few weeks, a federal grand jury would release its indictments. I calculated my chances of beating those charges were pretty slim. If convicted, I would simply run from the law and become a fugitive. The Cause demanded both service and sacrifice. I made preparations to flee and to live underground for as long as it took.

I returned to Mobile. Hoping to present a better image to the authorities, I took—and passed—the GED test, and enrolled in classes at Mobile College. I kept a low profile and gave every appearance of diligence in my studies.

I decided to take a trip by car to Los Angeles to deepen my ties with Dr. Wesley Swift, whose recorded sermons I had listened to back in Mobile. I also wanted to meet with other radical leaders on the West Coast. I talked with Dr. Swift by phone, and he invited me to come to California and serve as his understudy for a time. That was a surprising and flattering invitation, considering that I had never met him. But it would not be possible with federal firearms charges hanging over my head; a short visit would have to suffice.

I spent a fruitful week and a half getting acquainted with Dr. Swift and his aide, who was also the West Coast coordinator of the Minutemen, an anti-Communist organization. I had detailed discussions with them on ideology, strategy, and tactics—essentially how to organize resistance and conduct a terror campaign. We forged deep ties in the process.

Before returning home to Mobile, I went to San Diego to visit my favorite uncle, a former corporate vice president who now had his own business. He and his family visited Mobile every couple of years for summer vacation, and we all had a great time together. I had always enjoyed our visits. But this time it was very different. I had become so preoccupied with the Cause that it occupied all my thoughts and conversation. Nothing else interested me, and I had little else to talk about. Those who did not share my ideology and commitment were no longer a significant part of my life. I found that I had changed so much that my uncle and I had nothing in common anymore and could hardly communicate. I stayed only a day or two before driving back to Mobile.

*     *     *

On March 23, 1968, a warm, sunny day in Mobile, I decided to go down to Dauphin Island on the Gulf of Mexico to swim and get some sun. As I was returning home late that afternoon, I spotted FBI agents parked down the street, watching my parents' house. I had practiced for this, and now that training began to pay off. I quickly deduced that the federal indictment had come out and the agents were there to arrest me. My heart began to race wildly.

Instead of turning in to our driveway, I continued straight ahead as though I was just another neighbor on my way. Their car was facing mine, with the engine off, so I had to drive right past them. I looked straight ahead as if I hadn't noticed them.

But they recognized me. They jumped as though shocked by a cattle prod. I remember being surprised at how quickly their unmarked car started up. I punched the accelerator and sped away, my heart nearly in my mouth. They lost valuable time getting turned around on the narrow street. I made the corner well before they got their car straightened out. I made several fast turns, just as I had been trained, and I never saw them again.

The day I had long anticipated had arrived. I knew the entire Mobile police force would be looking for my car. I immediately went to the house of a close friend and changed cars. Then I made preparations for leaving the area quickly. Meanwhile, I learned that a team of FBI agents was searching my parents' house and questioning my family concerning my whereabouts, my plans, my friends, and my acquaintances. I knew the FBI would have needed a search warrant. That meant the agents were prepared to take me in. Knowing that steeled my resolve.

I had crossed over into a dark and darkening world. I was going underground. There was no going back now.

A few days later I was at a safe house in the mountains of North Carolina, where I could wait for the heat to subside. I stayed with a couple who were dedicated to the Cause. They were part of the Miami group that had scattered throughout the South. Like the others, they said little about what they had left behind or why. I fit right in.

I was no longer just a college student from Mobile. I was now a fugitive from justice.

*    *    *

While I was in North Carolina, news broke that Dr. Martin Luther King Jr. had been assassinated. This was a cause for celebration for many white Southern segregationists, for he was widely hated. For racists like me it meant that somewhere out there were others who were willing to take action. My North Carolina hosts and I watched the news with great interest as details emerged and law enforcement agencies searched for the killer. We were curious about who did it. We also hoped the killer would not be caught.

After several uneventful weeks, I decided to return secretly to Mississippi to meet with Sam Bowers. We discussed the political situation in the state and what the Klan's response should be. Over the course of a few days, I met with key people before returning to my hideout in North Carolina.

A few months later, during one of those meetings with a friend in a Jackson area restaurant, we heard news that Attorney General Robert Kennedy had been assassinated in Los Angeles. This provided further encouragement to all who hated the Kennedys. It showed that there were people outside of the South who were willing to take violent action against America's enemies. And it fed the tattered hope that we might win this struggle after all.

Throughout this time the Klan's reign of terror continued with machine-gun and bombing attacks on Jews and blacks. In Meridian alone there had been eleven terrorist acts since January, including the burning of eight black churches. May and June were particularly eventful months, and the state of Mississippi was crawling with federal agents. Thus, I spent most of that time in North Carolina.

Then in May of 1968, the Jewish synagogue in Meridian, Mississippi, was bombed. Tension and fear were at an all-time high. The FBI was intensely involved in investigating the situation, with J. Edgar Hoover receiving daily progress reports from the Meridian field office.

The Klan decided it was time for one very special operation. With great caution I returned to Mississippi in late June to coordinate the bombing of Meyer Davidson's house. The Cause was progressing, and this event would add to the work of others and advance it even more.

# OFF TO PRISON

The bombing of the Davidson home might have advanced the Cause at least temporarily had it succeeded. But its monumental failure turned out to be the death knell of the White Knights of the Ku Klux Klan in Mississippi. And that death knell was symbolized by my conviction.

I was sentenced on November 27, 1968, in Meridian. I returned to my cell, where I awaited my transfer to the Mississippi State Penitentiary—or Parchman prison, as most people called it. I knew where I was going, but I had no idea when.

December 13, 1968, was a cold and overcast day in Mississippi. Around lunchtime, the jailer told me to get ready to leave. After hurriedly packing the few things I had, I was taken out of my cell and handcuffed to a chain that was wrapped around my waist. Five other men, three white and two black, were similarly chained. I was added to the line of chained convicts.

We were taken downstairs to a prison station wagon used for transporting prisoners. The station wagon was specially equipped with wire-mesh screen covering the windows and forming a barrier between the driver and passengers. But because I was among those being transported, the Mississippi Highway Patrol had taken special measures to prevent my being rescued—or assassinated.

An entire convoy of Mississippi Highway Patrol cars escorted this prison wagon, leading our vehicle and following behind. Our speed was seldom less than eighty miles an hour. As we passed certain checkpoints, additional cars were waiting to relieve those that had been accompanying us. The gray skies added to my gloominess as we left Meridian. I said very little to my fellow prisoners.

The prison convoy proceeded north through the rolling hills around Philadelphia, Mississippi, as if on a tour of recent racial violence. It was here that Wayne Roberts and other Klan members had kidnapped and murdered the three civil rights workers: Chaney, Goodman, and Schwerner. From Philadelphia, we headed north to Kosciusko and then west toward Greenwood, the hometown of Byron De La Beckwith, who had been tried twice (with hung juries both times) for the murder of Medgar Evers.

Near Greenwood the terrain began to flatten out into the Mississippi Delta, one of the most fertile farming areas in the United States. I had never been to the Mississippi Delta until that day. As I looked at the passing fields, I felt a deep despair. All I could see were miles and miles of barrenness. Stark brown cotton stalks, already stripped by the pickers, dotted by a few white bolls of cotton that had been missed. Ramshackle shanties—often unpainted, with trash, weeds, and broken-down cars and appliances littering the yards—offered a sharp contrast to the occasional stately plantation-style home surrounded by well-manicured lawns and expensive cars in the driveways. The thousands of acres of cotton fields and soybeans belonged to the Delta farmers and planters who lived in these elegant houses. The field hands, sharecroppers, and tenant farmers occupied the shanties.

We drove across the Delta, with its fading remnants of the Old South juxtaposed with the new era of enormous, mechanized farms profiting from economies of scale. During the growing season this would all be green and lush under blue skies. But in mid-December it just looked brown and dead and gray. I felt as if I were approaching the outermost edges of the earth, as if I would soon be cut off from civilization altogether.

We reached Parchman, about ninety miles south of Memphis, Tennessee, just before dark. Unlike most prisons, which are compact, filled with cells, and surrounded by high walls, Parchman was a penal farm sprawling across eighteen thousand acres. It resembled a military reservation more than a prison.

Parchman was established in 1901. Its mission was to house and work state prisoners. Inmates worked the fields, growing cotton, soybeans, vegetables, and other crops, with the goal of making an annual profit for the prison. Military-style, barracks-like compounds were situated at various points on the farm. Prisoners were segregated by race. Each "camp" housed an average of 100 to 175 men. The large brick buildings contained two open dormitories, a kitchen, a dining hall, and bathing areas. Outside was a four- or five-acre yard large enough for football, baseball, and basketball. A twelve-foot, heavy-duty, chain-link fence topped with barbed concertina wire surrounded each camp. Guard towers stood on each corner.

The convoy drove past a brick guard station at the prison entrance, then proceeded down a two-lane, blacktop road called "guard row." On either side were frame "shotgun" houses, built in the 1930s, one right after another about a hundred feet apart. Here the guards and other employees lived in a sequestered community largely untouched by time and modern society. In some families, multiple generations had worked at the prison. I noticed how the windows and doors were decorated for Christmas with lights—red, green, yellow, white, and blue.

But for me, this season of joy would bring only depression, because

I could not be part of celebrating Christmas now or for years to come. I felt a deep pang of anguish as I recalled the many happy Christmases I had spent at home with my family in Mobile during my preteen years. I don't think I've ever felt a greater sense of aloneness and hopelessness than when we entered the prison grounds.

A little more than a mile down guard row, we reached the prison hospital, a large, old, one-story, red-brick building surrounded by a tall fence and guard towers. The gate was swung open just long enough for us to drive through, and then a guard locked it shut again. We were now securely in Parchman prison, long known as one of the worst in the United States. Hard labor and harsh conditions had been the norm since its founding. Farming in the blazing hot, smothering humidity of Mississippi summers and its chilling, wet winters was the lot of most prisoners, the vast majority of whom were black. Brutality was employed as needed to keep prisoners in line, and there was no recourse, even in the courts.

All new prisoners were processed at the hospital and given a medical exam. The six of us were led in chains into the reception area. The door was shut and locked behind us by the sergeant in charge of the hospital as well as the receiving officer. He was an abrupt person who said little, but when he spoke there was no doubt who was in charge. Our chains and handcuffs were removed.

We were ordered to line up side by side, strip naked, and put our clothes in a pile in front of us. Then we were made to assume various postures in order to permit a visual inspection. We even had to show the bottoms of our feet. Once the sergeant was satisfied that no one was concealing contraband on his person, we were each issued underwear, towels, three pairs of jeans, and three khaki shirts. Next, we were told to put on our new prison clothes. Everyone except me had all his hair cut off. Was it an oversight? Or perhaps a favor from someone who approved of my racist views? I never understood why I was spared this part of the induction ritual.

For supper, we were directed to the dining hall in the back of the hospital. The food was surprisingly good, much better than in the Lauderdale County Jail. There was fresh milk, meat, bread, and vegetables. After supper we were given blood tests and a routine physical examination and then placed in the sick ward of the hospital.

Later that night, after my own processing had been completed, I was taken to the maximum-security unit, or MSU, known as "Little Alcatraz." I had assumed I would remain at the hospital with the other prisoners pending assignment to a camp. However, because of my notoriety, prison officials were taking no chances with me. They didn't want me to escape. They didn't want anyone to kill me either. The MSU was the safest place for me.

It was a well-lit concrete, brick, and steel building located in a flat, barren area surrounded by its own twelve-foot fence topped with barbed wire and tall, brick guard towers on each corner. It looked sinister and forbidding. It represented isolation, even from the prison itself. When we reached the entrance to the compound, the huge electric gate slowly rolled open, closing again as soon as our car entered. We were now in what could be described as a fenced-in box. A hundred feet beyond the entrance was another gate. Once the guards placed their guns in a depository, the second gate opened and we were allowed to pass through and into the grounds.

The MSU building was a long, one-story, red-brick structure with a low, flat roof. The entrance was in the middle of the building, dividing it into two wings, east and west. A row of barred eighteen-inch windows ran the length of the building just below its roof line. Access to the building was through an electronically operated door of heavy steel grating. This opened into an office and central control area that separated the two wings. Each wing had two cellblocks. Solid steel doors led into the cellblocks on either side of each wing.

I was taken into the receiving area and again made to strip naked.

But this time I was also made to spread my legs apart and bend over for further inspection. All my newly issued prison clothes were taken, and I was given a set of long underwear and a blanket. I was then escorted by staff and trusties to cell 13 at the very end of death row, which was a cellblock on one of the wings. I got an eerie feeling as I walked down the cellblock corridor with men looking out at me from each cell as I passed. We stopped near the end. Slowly the cell door rolled open, and I went inside. Then it shut with a solid, foreboding clang. There I stood, with the gas chamber and all its horrors as my neighbor.

The cellblock consisted of a ten-foot-wide corridor about a hundred feet long, beginning with a double shower stall and followed by thirteen cells, one after another, opening into the corridor. Each cell was a concrete cubicle approximately six by nine feet with gray steel bars across the front and a sliding door operated from a control panel at the entrance to the cellblock. A six-inch-thick, concrete wall separated each cell. The building's narrow row of windows ran the length of the cellblock along the top of the corridor wall across from the cells. The upper half of the walls was painted white and the lower half light green. The floor was plain concrete. Seven or eight incandescent 150-watt light bulbs were spaced along the corridor ceiling.

Although this was death row, only five of the men actually had death sentences pending. The others were ordinary prisoners who had to be locked up for their own safety or because they were escape risks, both of which were the case for me.

The other three cellblocks in the maximum-security unit were used for safekeeping or punishment. Before my arrival at Parchman, officials were reported to have sent prisoners they regarded as disciplinary problems to the MSU. Here they would be locked in a cell without a mattress or cover—only a bare steel bunk, commode, and face bowl. In those days, the starvation diet, reserved for hard cases, consisted of two meals a day: a cup of coffee and two biscuits with sorghum molasses for breakfast and a one-inch square of corn bread and one teaspoon of black-eyed peas for supper. Especially troublesome individuals were placed in "the dark hole," a six-foot-square cell, completely enclosed, and pitch dark when the door was shut. They received only water and a slight food ration. Toilet facilities were built into the floor and consisted of an eight-inch hole level with the floor, which could be flushed by a button on the wall.

Although officials had largely phased out harsh discipline of unruly prisoners by the time of my incarceration, there were still occasional reports of what could be considered excessive punishment. The inmates on the cellblock where I was housed had been there for years and told me stories of what it was like in the "old days." During the winter, officials might use a garden hose to spray everyone down until they were soaking wet, then open the windows and turn on the powerful overhead exhaust fan. The effect of the strong draft of cold air on wet bodies was highly effective. A few hours of this treatment would quiet down even the hardest and toughest of men. During the summer, the technique was reversed. The exhaust fans, which normally ran day and night during the summer, were turned off. The hot-box effect then served equally well to subdue the unruly.

In some cases, officials and trusties would even enter the cells of certain "hard cases" and beat the men down with blackjacks, a type of weapon consisting of leather-enclosed metal with a strap for a handle. They would give a strong laxative to others and handcuff them to the bars of their cells with their hands stuck so high up on the crossbars that they had to stand on tiptoe. Once the laxative took effect, it was an extremely miserable situation. Every time a man was sent to the maximum-security unit for punishment, his head was shaved before he was taken to his cell.

These things were common until about the time I came, in 1968. As late as 1964, men were regularly whipped with "the bull hide"—also called "Black Annie." This was a leather strap one-quarter of an inch thick and about six inches wide and four feet long. Usually ten hard licks would be administered to the naked buttocks of a man while four trusties held him down, one on each arm and leg. The "hide" was dreaded by all and could tame anyone.

Fortunately, the official policy of the new superintendent, Tom Cook, discontinued corporal punishment. Some of the hard-line, old-guard officials still tried to use these methods occasionally but could rarely get away with it.

There was often conversation among the prisoners along the cellblock. Not long after I had settled down in my cell, the man in cell 12 told me that he was being held for "safekeeping." He had previously been in prison in Louisiana. He asked my name and where I was from. He then passed the word to the others in the cellblock. Everyone knew about me, of course, because they had been reading the newspaper and listening to the radio. They treated me like a celebrity. Word had spread that I was a top Klan terrorist who had shot a policeman (with a submachine gun, no less) in a wild gun battle. They were surprised to discover that I was quiet, reserved, and aloof. And unlike some, I didn't talk about my crime.

Of the five men with death sentences, three were black and the other two white. The remaining six who were there for safekeeping were evenly divided racially. They were housed on death row because they had escaped or were in protective custody. One fellow was a psychiatric case and was awaiting transfer to the state mental hospital. Another had escaped and been recaptured. Another had informed on someone and had to be locked up for his own protection.

I was confined to my cell twenty-four hours a day—as was everyone else on death row. Twice a week we were allowed out for fifteen to thirty minutes to shower and shave. It was a very restrictive existence. The cell itself was a drab, dismal place, reminiscent of a stall in a dog kennel. The concrete walls were covered with graffiti—names of those who had been in the cell and the dates, curse words, lewd comments, maxims, and so forth. The commode and face bowl, once white porcelain, were dull, stained, and dirty. A dirty mattress lay on the steel-frame bunk, and a large, heavy quilt provided warm covering. Otherwise the cell was as bare as the smooth concrete floor.

In a short time, I realized that boredom—with nowhere to go and nothing to do—was one of the worst aspects of this type of prison life. It is a very difficult adjustment for a normal, energetic person. My activities were limited to talking, reading, and thinking, all of which grew old quickly. I could not help but do a lot of thinking. This produced frustration and despair or self-pity, as I thought back on my earlier life and how good it had been in comparison to what I was now experiencing. Simple things that I took for granted when I was free now appeared to me in a very different light. Something as simple as going to the grocery store seemed a wonderful thing compared to sitting in a six-by-nine-foot cell. I wished that I had never gotten myself into such a terrible situation. Why couldn't I have found a different way to help the Cause, a way that wouldn't have gotten me into prison? But it was now too late. I was reaping what I had sown. But my commitment to the Cause was undiminished.

To temporarily escape from the unpleasant reality of their cells and their boredom, prisoners listened to music on small portable radios and absorbed themselves in reading material—usually westerns and murder mysteries.

When you are locked up, little things you once took for granted become much more important. And nowhere was that truer than with food. The sameness of daily meals only increased the boredom. Breakfast, served at about 6:00 a.m., consisted of either hotcakes, bacon, oatmeal, and molasses or eggs, grits, sausage, biscuits, and peach preserves, with all the milk and coffee one could drink. The afternoon meal, served around 3:00 p.m., usually consisted of pork or beef in some form, corn bread, canned vegetables—such as turnips, Irish potatoes, yams, beans, or squash—a dessert, and milk. Various fresh fruits and vegetables were also served in season. But the menu changed little.

My stay on death row was short, lasting less than two weeks. No doubt it would have been much longer had it not been for an incident that occurred about ten days after my arrival. On December 23, 1968, three days after my twenty-second birthday, I was in low spirits when super-intendent Tom Cook and two chaplains, Rev. W. D. Kirk and Rev. Selby McManus, came in to give everyone a Christmas gift and hold a brief service. They had been in the cellblock only a few minutes when one of the inmates began heatedly shouting. He and others were angry about what they felt was the low quality of the meals being served at Parchman.

A few minutes later, I heard sounds of porcelain shattering against the bars and out in the corridor. In an angry rage, one of the men had somehow kicked his toilet loose from the wall and was throwing the bro-ken pieces at the warden and chaplains. Others immediately followed his lead as the warden and chaplains fled to safety. A few minutes later, smoke began filtering down the corridor from mattresses that had been set afire with the matches the men used to light their cigarettes. The guards quickly activated the powerful ventilator system and flooded the cellblock with water. This brought the would-be riot under control.

About an hour later, after the fury had subsided, the sergeant in charge of the maximum-security unit walked down the corridor to assess the damage. All but three toilets in the cellblock had been destroyed, broken up, and used as missiles.

When the sergeant came to my cell, he saw that it was intact and orderly. I had not participated in the riot. Even if I had known about the grievance and the intended protest (which I did not), I would not have taken part. Such an effort was absolutely futile and hadn't the slightest chance of producing any positive gains. Besides, I had never been one to follow the herd. In addition, I had been raised to respect older people and those in authority and was basically pro law enforcement. My defiance of authority started when they began to enforce desegregation and civil rights laws, which I saw as un-American.

Because I did not join the riot, the warden transferred me and two other men to the hospital unit, the second most secure place at the prison, where I was given a job as a laboratory technician trainee. In spite of my notoriety, he wanted to give me a chance to prove myself suitable for a less restrictive custody classification.

# PRISON LIFE

M y transfer to the hospital unit was an unexpected boon. Although the security was tighter than any other unit of the prison except maximum security, the general living conditions were much better than elsewhere at Parchman.

I was housed in a small dormitory with about a dozen other inmates who worked at the hospital. Our room had its own TV and bathroom and was fairly comfortable, although short on space. It was cleaner than any of the other camps, and the food was better. The man in charge of the hospital, Sergeant Paul Miller, could be intimidating at times but was a decent guy, which made things better still.

During the six months I spent at the hospital unit, my parents drove from Mobile almost every visiting day (the first and third Sundays of the month) to spend two hours with me. Although their separation had by now turned into divorce, they had a civil relationship. My parents both worked, and the trip was quite a strain on them, getting up at 4:00 a.m.

on a Sunday morning, driving the 325 miles to Parchman, then turning around after two hours and driving back, arriving home after midnight. Each time they came, they brought my favorite snack foods and magazines. Seeing my parents so often encouraged me and helped keep up my morale. We talked about how things were at home, how various family members were doing, and, of course, my situation. Their visits reminded me that there was hope and that the horrible prison environment did not have to define me.

My girlfriend was not allowed to visit me, and I realized that there was no future for our relationship. I wrote her a letter explaining the realities of my situation, which of course she knew all too well, and encouraged her to forget about me and move on with her life. It was hard to do, but it was the right thing.

\*     \*     \*

My work at the prison as a laboratory technician was completely foreign to me. I didn't particularly like it, but it was a good job in terms of the fringe benefits (i.e., living at the hospital), so I learned quickly. My teacher was another inmate who had held the job for several years and was soon to be paroled. Although this journeyman-apprentice approach was rather crude in such a complicated field, I learned the basics fairly well in a short time, and basics were all that were required.

My workday consisted of breakfast at 5:00 a.m., then routine laboratory procedures—urinalyses, white-cell counts, hemoglobin, hematocrit, glucose tolerance, and other testing. Each new inmate entering the prison was also blood-typed and tested for venereal disease. Occasionally I performed an EKG.

My work brought me into daily contact with the prison's physician, Dr. Luther McCaskill, who was an inmate himself. He had been convicted of performing an illegal abortion on a woman who later died from complications. Dr. McCaskill was black and in his early forties. His jovial personality and genuine compassion earned him the respect of the inmates and staff alike.

Although he knew my background of racism and violence, it did not matter to him. He befriended me. My friendship with "Dr. Mac" began to alter my racial views. He was the first black person I knew as an adult. It was racist ideology meeting reality. I knew all the negative stereotypes about blacks, but in front of me was a real human being who broke those stereotypes. As we came to know each other better, my hard attitudes about blacks softened. I found myself liking him more and more. There was no denying that he was a smart, highly educated, and kindhearted man. He certainly didn't fit the stereotypes in racist literature I had been fed. Although we never discussed my background or racial issues, I am sure such conversations would have helped my views change even faster.

Dr. Mac provided me with the best medical treatment he could on a number of occasions, especially during the periodic episodes of acute pain in my arm from the gunshot wounds. When the pain was really intense, he would prescribe a non-narcotic painkilling drug to bring relief. He could have easily told me to take some aspirin (which would not have helped) and sent me on my way, leaving me to endure intense pain. But he didn't. Goodwill and friendship like this began breaking down my prejudices and stereotypes just a little bit.

In those days, Parchman prison operated under what was called the "trusty system." This system, which was established in the early 1900s, allowed inmates selected by prison officials to serve either as armed guards and supervisors of other inmates, or as clerks, janitors, and so on. The armed trusties were called "shooters" because they carried guns and functioned as civilian guards. Unarmed trusties were simply called "trusties." In return for their services, trusties were given special privileges and enjoyed considerable freedom. With special permission from the camp sergeant, trusties might come and go on prison grounds without an escort, could drive prison vehicles, and could fish or hunt on the grounds during off-duty hours. Trusties also had special living quarters, separate from the other inmates, and were never locked up. Each year at Christmas they were allowed to go home on a ten-day holiday leave. Another perk was that they were generally fed better than other prisoners and were permitted items that others were denied for security reasons. In short, being a trusty made prison life more bearable.

Selected by the camp sergeant and approved by the superintendent or assistant superintendent, a trusty could be stripped of his rank at the discretion of the sergeant, with little recourse available. This served to make trusties dependent on the sergeant's goodwill and produced an almost unquestioning obedience to his orders—right or wrong. This was doubly reinforced because when a trusty was stripped of his status, he was placed back into the regular prison population—with the very men he had guarded and sometimes mistreated.

Life was not easy for the rank-and-file prisoners at Parchman prison, most of whom were black. Since it was a penal farm, most inmates were compelled to do farm work. This chiefly consisted of planting, hoeing, and harvesting cotton and various vegetable crops. Most of the work was done by hand. Only in the midsixties did tractors and mechanical cotton pickers begin to slowly replace manual labor. Often one could see a line of 100 to 150 men moving through a field side by side, picking or hoeing cotton. Arduous labor continued relentlessly year-round—from daylight to dark, five and a half days a week, often in a hundred-plus-degree temperatures in summer to twenty-degree temperatures in winter.

The inmates, quite naturally, hated the system. Sometimes they refused to work, and other times they would work slowly. And some just could not keep up with the grueling pace and rigorous conditions. To speed up those who worked slowly—and to coerce those who stopped—trusties would sometimes fire rifle rounds in the prisoners' vicinity. Occasionally men would be hit by this rifle fire, usually because of poor

aim or a ricochet, but sometimes it was deliberate. Not until the late sixties, when I arrived, did these conditions change.

The wounded were brought to the hospital for treatment and then
sent back to work the field as soon as possible. Most of the serious injuries
were the result of conflicts among the inmates themselves. This was pri-
marily what I saw and helped treat. These incidents frequently originated
from drunken arguments or same-sex relationships.

Drinking was a periodic problem. There were prisoners in every camp
devoted to the manufacture and sale of home brew. This was usually
made by fermenting potatoes or apples or raisins in a solution of sugar
and water. After three or four days, a potent beverage resulted. Yeast was
used when available to speed the process and improve the product. It was
a constant matching of wits for the inmates to find the containers, raw
materials, and places to make their home brew, but somehow they succeeded. Often kitchen personnel made the home brew, or at least helped,
because they had access to the needed supplies. Brew was found everywhere from footlockers to attics to holes carefully dug and camouflaged
in the yard. Containers ranged from cooking pots to wash pails and mop
buckets. On one occasion, someone even used a high-topped rubber boot.

Prison officials were always on the lookout for home brew because it
caused so much trouble. In the tensely charged atmosphere of a prison,
drinking was dangerous. It lowered inhibitions to the point where hostile
impulses were more readily expressed. I remember one instance in which
a man was stabbed in the chest and abdomen. Someone apparently had
tried to steal the affections of his boyfriend. In the ensuing fight, the
man was almost killed. In a similar situation, an inmate was attacked in
his sleep and beaten on the head with a heavy iron bar. He miraculously
survived but with permanent blindness.

One day as I was working in the lab, two men from one of the camps
were rushed to the emergency room, with Dr. Mac close at hand. As they
were being wheeled down the corridor, blood was spurting everywhere.

One was the camp's cook and the other its baker. They had been drinking and got into a fight with long, sharp butcher knives. The cook's arm was laid open like a ham that had been boned. His nerves and tendons had been severed, and his arm was just hanging. The baker, barely alive, had been stabbed in the chest and abdomen and was gushing blood. Fortunately, Dr. Mac's medical skill helped both to survive, although each required several operations before becoming well again.

Because any inmate (except those in maximum security) could come to the hospital for sick call, it was the central point for drug transactions. The drugs were obtained by theft from the pharmacy, by purchases or gifts from patients for whom they were prescribed, or from visitors of inmates.

Because the hospital was my initial assignment, I was able to avoid some of the more difficult challenges of adjustment. Here I found a more intelligent, higher caliber of inmates and much less peer pressure than in the other camps, where conformity to the group was necessary not only for acceptance but also for personal security.

Generally, new inmates adopted the attitudes (feigned or unfeigned) of the prison subculture toward society, staff, and other inmates. This was necessary for survival in such a hostile environment, but unfortunately it held dire consequences for readjustment after release from prison. Many of those who become acculturated to prison life are not aware that they have these attitudes and values when they return to the free world. Inevitably their ways of thinking and behaving produce conflict and difficulty in their dealings with others—family, friends, and employers. In addition, a person's emotional development is substantially slowed while he is in prison. Thus, released inmates often have a hard time readjusting to normal society. This often leads to situations that assure their return to prison—where the behaviors are further reinforced. More than two-thirds commit another crime within three years and are returned to prison.[1]

Fortunately, I did not fall into this trap, partly because of my being at the hospital but also because I never really adapted to the prison subculture. Terrible things can and do happen to people in prison. It is often a dehumanizing environment that makes people worse. But the hospital unit was safe, and it was one of the best places I could have been. Being there kept me from being exposed to the harsh and dangerous side of prison life.

# BIDING MY TIME AND PREPARING

In spite of appearances, I was not adjusting to prison life at the hospital unit. Although my friendship with Dr. Mac had broken through my stereotypes, that was just the first step of what would be a long journey. My racism was still intact, and my commitment to the Cause was as strong as ever. And I had no intention of remaining at Parchman. Just like a captured combatant in the military, I considered it my duty to escape, evade being recaptured, and rejoin the war. I was merely biding my time while analyzing the security system for weaknesses. Once I gained a thorough working knowledge of the prison's general security operations and of the hospital in particular, I began planning my escape.

One of the reasons prison officials, most of whom shared my racial and political views, trusted me was my attitude toward them. I respected them and readily accepted their authority. This contrasted with the majority of inmates, whose attitudes were resentful toward authority in general, and particularly toward prison authority. As a result of my

attitude toward them, prison officials grew more confident in their attitude toward me.

Although I was friendly to the officials and liked some of them, I
refused to stay in prison. I believed that the United States was still being
undermined by the Communist-Jewish conspiracy. I needed to break out
and get back in the thick of the battle against it. Many people seemed to
be content to study and speak out about it. I felt that the time had come
for action, to press the terror campaign against America's enemies until
it caught on elsewhere.

I concluded that a successful escape would require the assistance of
one or two other inmates within the hospital. The first person was not
hard to find. Louis Shadoan was a clerk in his midforties who worked the
identification office and was very intelligent. He had worked as a jour-
nalist, but his real profession was robbing banks. He was quite good at it,
having robbed several in the Midwest. Moreover, Louis was looking at a
long time in prison—when he finished his sentence at Parchman, he was
to be transferred to a federal prison for violating his parole on a separate
bank robbery charge.

Overall, Louis seemed like a solid potential recruit who could be
trusted. He agreed to join me in an escape. We quietly began our planning
in his office. We observed the day-to-day operation of the hospital unit,
noting in detail the times and manner of garbage pickup, supply deliveries,
changing of the guard, and so forth. The hospital closed at 5:00 p.m., and
until five the next morning there was only one prison employee on duty in
the compound. This particular guard was in his fifties and was slow, quiet,
short, and slightly overweight. We determined the route of least resistance
would be to overpower him late one evening and to bribe one or more of
the trusties working as outside tower guards.

Once we had formulated the basic plan, we moved into more intensive planning. The escape would have three distinct phases. First, we
had to leave the hospital compound safely; second, we had to reach a

secure hideout; finally, we would split up and go our separate ways to final destinations.

Plans for implementing phase one went smoothly. Louis cultivated a rapport with the trusty on one of the two front guard towers with the intention of bribing him at the proper time. I contacted a reliable inmate I knew and secured a map of the terrain and roads around the eighteen-thousand-acre (twenty-eight-square-miles) prison farm. With this we could plan for our pickup. Louis and I then began compiling a list of supplies we would need once we were free. Arms, ammunition, hand grenades, food, clothing, camping gear, and other items, such as radio monitoring equipment and medical supplies, were all included.

I established and maintained contact with a close Klan colleague by smuggling letters in and out through an inmate's family. The Klan member and another friend began securing the supplies right away from sporting stores and surplus centers.

The second phase, getting from the prison grounds to our hideout, presented no problems at all in my mind. My Klan friends made trips to the Parchman area to reconnoiter the prison grounds and the hospital unit. On one of these reconnaissance missions, one of them made his way through the fields to within a stone's throw of the hospital compound. On another occasion, one of them had car trouble some forty miles from the prison. County sheriff's deputies, the highway patrol, and the FBI investigated but apparently did not connect the incident with any planned escape from Parchman.

Our prison break was going to be a tricky operation. Everything had to work as planned or we might well be killed. As Louis and I continued to plan our escape, we both recognized the need for a third person to assure adequate manpower in taking over the hospital. Anything less might increase the chance of resistance on the part of the guards and night watchman. After careful consideration, we decided that we could safely approach Malcolm Houston, a thirtysomething inmate orderly in one of the wards. Since he had attempted to escape before, we felt that he would be interested. Louis, who knew him better than I, made the initial approach and found Malcolm receptive. Then I talked with him. We both felt that he was the man we needed and included him in our plans.

By this time, our accomplices in the free world had secured all needed supplies, carefully reconnoitered the prison area, and secured a safe place for our hideout—an old abandoned farm in a heavily wooded, rural area just outside Jackson, Mississippi.

All we needed to do now was coordinate the time of our pickup. This was a crucial part of the plan. We had to know for sure that they would be at the rendezvous point before making our break. Because unforeseen developments might arise to keep them from being there, we had to confirm it on the day of the escape. Phone calls in or out of the prison were forbidden in those days. We had to devise an alternative means of communication. Smuggled letters were too slow, and walkie-talkies were too risky. A newspaper was the only other source of daily communication accessible to us. So, we decided that they would place a classified ad in the *Jackson Daily News*, an evening paper, on the day they would be at the rendezvous point. If placed early in the morning, the ad would appear in the afternoon edition, which was delivered to the hospital each day. The ad would be innocent to everyone but Louis and me; it would read: "Lost: German shepherd. Name Sam. Black and silver in color. Large size," with a specific phone number. This would be our signal that they would be at the spot that night.

Even if they were able to be at the rendezvous point, unforeseeable developments within the prison might still prevent us from attempting an escape. We needed some flexibility in the schedule, so we set three consecutive days for my friends to be waiting for us. If we did not make our break the first night, then we could fall back on the second or third. They would be there each night. But what if there were unforeseeable developments on their end that kept them from being there? There was no way for them to alert us. If that happened, we would be sitting ducks for the well-armed prison search teams and vulnerable to whatever they decided to do to us. This was a big risk, but we decided to take our chances. We were so far into our planning and our relishing of the idea of freedom that it was hard to turn back.

# 11
# ESCAPE!

Nothing compares to a hot, muggy day in Mississippi.

Wednesday, July 23, 1969, was a classic day of summer heat in the Magnolia State, and it was the first of three possible days for our escape. I was grateful for the heat and the humidity, as it covered any nervous perspiration I was generating. I needed to be seen doing my business-as-usual routine. Inwardly, I was on edge, but was buoyed by the pleasant thought that this would be my last day in prison. Soon I would be free—and eventually active in the Cause again.

The escape would be dangerous. There was no avoiding the risk that we might get captured and/or shot. I was tense. But I was also confident in my skill, planning, and competence. I had anticipated possible problems, planned appropriately, and did not doubt that we could succeed—if all went as planned.

Several times that morning I pushed my chair away from the desk and walked down to Louis's office to check in. A little later, I went to Malcolm's desk in the patient ward. These visits were short because the doctor sent patients to me for tests throughout the day. We could not afford an extended discussion or the attention it might attract. All of us tried to be inconspicuous, but it seemed as if the hours would never pass. As morning gave way to afternoon, the tension and excitement increased. I waited expectantly for the newspaper to arrive.

It was close to 5:00 p.m., and the newspaper hadn't been delivered. Time stood still. We continued to wait, but still no paper. We were ready to move as soon as it got dark, but until we saw the paper, we had no way of knowing whether anyone would be there to pick us up. If we escaped and got to the rendezvous point and they were not there, we would surely be recaptured, if not killed. Our predicament was critical. If the paper was not delivered soon, we would have to switch to another night. We anxiously waited.

On a normal day, a trusty assigned to a paper route delivered news-papers for subscribers at all the camps, homes, and administrative buildings on the farm. Finally, he came with the two or three copies that were delivered to the hospital. Louis asked to look at one and came by my office with it under his arm. I saw it, got up quickly, and followed him to his office, where we nervously scanned the classifieds.

The ad was there. They would be waiting for us.

Now we were ready for the final countdown. Louis immediately went to the head cook, a trusted friend, and got the keys to the kitchen, which had been locked up since suppertime. He sneaked into the kitchen unobserved and got three large butcher knives, one for each of us. We concealed these beneath our clothing just a few minutes before we were scheduled to be locked into our dormitories along with everyone else. Malcolm and I were in one dorm, and Louis was in the other.

The dorms were hot and stuffy. The air conditioning was poor in the crowded room—six double bunks in a space of about fifteen square feet. Now I was sweating freely. I kept glancing at my watch. A minute seemed like an hour.

Looking out the window, I could see the shadows growing long in the humid stillness of the evening. Although the heat was stifling, it was a beautiful summer evening in the Mississippi Delta as the sun sank below the horizon.

Freedom was calling. That was even more beautiful.

Around 8:00 p.m. the night watchman, who would normally unlock the door to our dorm and come give medicine to those scheduled to get it, came. When the door opened, Malcolm and I were waiting. We flashed the butcher knives at both the portly watchman and the trusty who assisted him and quietly told them that they would not be hurt if they cooperated with us. The sight of the large, ugly knives struck terror into both men, who assured us they would do as we said if we would not hurt them. We then crossed the hall and let Louis out of his dormitory, locking both dorms behind us and taking the night watchman with us.

We took the watchman's keys from his pocket, then tied up both men with wide adhesive tape that we had secured in advance from the emergency room. So far everything was perfect. Even the other prisoners in our dorm were unaware of what had happened. We quickly went to the front hall of the hospital, where the intercom system and night watchman's desk were located. This was the most critical and dangerous stage of the whole operation. Failure here would doom us.

First, we called our trusty friend in from the front tower. Louis had already told him that this would be the night. He came right in as if everything was normal, and we tied him up with tape. Next, we called in the only other guard in the front area of the compound. Because it often was difficult to distinguish voices over the intercom, he also came in unsuspecting. This was not too unusual. Guards were often summoned in from their posts. Louis hit him over the head from behind, momentarily stunning him. After he regained his balance and composure, he saw the knives and offered no resistance. Louis and Malcolm then tied him up also.

With everything secure inside the compound and no guards to stop us, the three of us openly and casually walked out the gate to the parking area, got into the watchman's car, and drove off. About a mile down a dirt road that cut through a cotton field, we reached an irrigation creek where the bridge was washed out, which we had known about in advance. We were more than a mile from the rendezvous point and could go no farther by car. Our intent was to leave the watchman's vehicle behind to decoy prison officials into thinking we were afoot in the general vicinity, diverting their attention to the wooded areas nearby instead of the highways on which we would be traveling.

After years and years of chasing escapees through the same terrain, officials had the art of pursuit down to a science. As soon as our escape was discovered, the alert would go out to all prison personnel, highway patrolmen, and sheriff's deputies in the area. Prison officials would immediately move out in radio-equipped cars and pickup trucks to preassigned checkpoints in an effort to seal off the area. Since the delta was so flat and had so few trees, men at key positions with binoculars, walkie-talkies, and rifles could command a wide view. They often spotted escapees running through the fields. Moreover, the prison's pack of well-trained bloodhounds would immediately be on the trail. It was absolutely essential that we quickly reach the getaway car and clear the area as quickly as possible.

Every minute was important. Success or failure would be determined by how quickly we reached the rendezvous point a mile away. We were soaked in sweat from the sweltering heat and high humidity. We waded across the creek, a distance of some thirty feet in waist-high water. Because of the soft, muddy bottom, it was slow going. Each step sank us to the ankles in thick, gummy mud.

Once clear of the creek, we ran through fields of young cotton plants. Our eyes burned as sweat combined with the cotton dust trickled into our eyes. None of us had exercised much in the previous months, and it showed.

We had run about half a mile when we began tiring. Louis and Malcolm had fallen behind, and I was exhausted. My stomach muscles ached. My soggy shoes and trousers seemed to weigh a hundred pounds. We slowed to a more moderate pace. It seemed as if we would never reach the rendezvous point ahead. Life and death hung in the balance.

My chest ached and my heart beat wildly. Yet somehow I kept going and encouraged the others that we were almost there. Finally, we saw the rendezvous point ahead of us.

It had taken longer than planned to get there. We didn't see anyone waiting. Had our rescuers not come after all—or had they left already? For the first time in the escape, actual fear struck my heart. I called out their names as loudly as I could. No answer.

Again, I called. Still no answer.

I hadn't planned for this. A wave of panic swept over me.

Then suddenly, out of nowhere, our rescuers emerged from a clump of woods where they had been concealed, listening to the monitoring radio in the car. They were extremely anxious.

"Hurry! Somebody saw you leave the hospital, and the alert has been on the air for at least ten minutes." That meant vehicles were already on the way to seal off the area.

Every second was vital.

We piled into the getaway car. There was a virtual arsenal in the car— multiple pistols, several automatic rifles, even a sack of hand grenades. We were each given a gun.

And then we were off, heading down the dirt road that would take us to the highway. We could hear the prison radio frequency crackling with directives and responses. Everything seemed to be going well. The search team had taken our bait with the watchman's car, concentrating their manpower in that area. Meanwhile we were putting valuable distance between us and them.

Suddenly a pair of headlights appeared in the distance behind us, moving at a high speed. We had to assume it was one of the prison vehicles. We sped up. But it was gaining on us.

Our driver accelerated even more, which was a dangerous move. Driving fast on dirt roads is tricky. It's easy to lose control. It would be a terrible wreck. Somehow the car held the road and stirred up so much dust that we lost the prison vehicle.

We reached a main highway about five miles south of the prison. From here we headed to the city of Greenwood. As we continued to monitor the highway patrol and prison frequencies, we learned that officials were still searching the prison area. But before we reached Greenwood, officials started blocking off roads. So, when we came into the city, we traveled through residential areas instead of using main thoroughfares.

As a precaution, Malcolm, Louis, and I got out of the car and hid in some brush while our friends checked the highway for roadblocks. About thirty minutes later they returned for us and we drove on to Canton, Mississippi, about seventy miles farther south. We repeated the same hide-and-seek precaution there. We arrived at the hideout at about 2:00 a.m., exhausted but safe.

We were free. My plan had worked! Less than one year after being sent to one of the most notorious penitentiaries in the United States, I had planned and led a successful breakout. I was exultant.

My euphoria would be short-lived.

# 12
# MAXIMUM SECURITY—AGAIN

News of my prison escape was quickly picked up by the news media around the Southeast, and instantly flashed to Meridian, where police chief Roy Gunn "freaked out," according to his friends. Fearing I was on a mission of personal retribution and revenge against him, Chief Gunn activated the entire city police force. He assigned half of the officers to protect his house around the clock.

The Roberts brothers, Raymond and Alton Wayne, who had set me up to be ambushed by the Meridian police, asked Chief Gunn for police protection, but he replied that he didn't have the manpower. So both of the Roberts brothers went into hiding.

Our hideout was an old, unoccupied farmhouse and barn on a large tract of land situated in a heavily wooded area about two miles from the Jackson municipal airport, known as Hawkins Field. Because the barn was farther from the road, we set up operations there. It was an old structure with straw scattered around the floor. A faint smell of old hay hung in the air. In some spots you could see daylight between the wooden siding boards.

We unloaded all our gear and weapons into the barn. Our rescuers left, returning the next night with hot food and more supplies. Louis, Malcolm, and I each took turns standing watch while the others slept.

When day broke, we prepared some breakfast. We had ample supplies of surplus army C rations and smokeless cooking fuel. I scouted out the general area to determine the proximity of roads, houses, water supplies, and so forth. The remainder of the day was uneventful, and when not standing watch, we slept or discussed the next phase of the escape. Louis would go to California and Malcolm would go to New Orleans. I wanted to immediately resume my activities for the Cause, but I would have to go into hiding for a while somewhere far away.

That night, one of our accomplices brought us some hot food. He was accompanied by a woman I had never seen before. I wasn't happy. It was an inexcusable breach of security.

"Who is this woman? Why did you bring her here?" I demanded.

"She's my fiancée, and she's totally trustworthy. Don't worry. Everything will be fine," he replied.

I was furious. I had a very bad feeling about the "fiancée." But there was nothing more I could say.

We got down to the business at hand. We discussed arrangements to get Malcolm and Louis on their respective ways. With them gone, I would feel much better. Then I would be able to make plans for my own departure. As I listened to the radio, I smiled. Each radio news broadcast had less to say about our escape.

The next morning was the third day since our escape from Parchman. The sweltering summer heat and humidity continued. We had no running water, no showers or toilets. I was feeling grubby from not bathing. I was worn-out from lack of sleep. We decided to move out of the barn and set up a tent in some heavy underbrush nearby. It reduced the chances of anyone either stumbling upon us or trapping us in the barn.

I stood watch throughout the heat of the afternoon and into the muggy evening. About 7:00 p.m. Louis came up to relieve me. He was half an hour early. I walked back to the tent, checked the monitoring radio, and immediately fell into a deep sleep. I had been asleep in the tent for maybe five or ten minutes when I was jolted awake by the loud staccato booms of gunfire. I sat up in a daze. We were in the middle of a pitched gun battle.

Malcolm looked at me in utter bewilderment. As we gathered our senses, we realized the gunshots were coming from out near the road where Louis was standing watch—about seventy-five feet away. Malcolm and I raced out of the tent and took cover behind a fallen tree. Despite being armed with automatic weapons and hand grenades, neither of us fired a shot. We were too confused. The assault team had achieved total surprise.

Out of nowhere a helicopter appeared and hovered overhead. Just as suddenly the shooting stopped.

"This is Roy Moore with the FBI," announced a voice over a bullhorn. "Shadoan is dead and you are surrounded. I am giving you one chance to surrender."

The police were armed with rifles, shotguns, submachine guns, and grenade launchers. To flee was impossible. Resistance would have been fatal. We had no choice but to surrender.

We came out of our hiding place with our hands high in the air. We were at once rushed by at least twenty FBI agents and state police. They ordered us to strip naked, placed us on the ground, and searched us thoroughly. We quickly dressed, and our captors tied our hands behind our backs with plastic zip-tie strips. They marched us right past Louis's bullet-riddled body.

One of the agents made me stop and look. He pointed and said, "See what you caused!" It was a horrible sight.

He was right. Had Louis Shadoan not followed my lead on this escape attempt, he'd still be alive. Had he not been so generous as to relieve me half an hour early, the bullet-riddled body would have been mine.

With that thought burning in my brain, Malcolm Houston and I were loaded into FBI cars and began the 140-mile trip back to Parchman.

\*　　\*　　\*

The caravan of FBI cars pulled into Parchman late that night. Malcolm and I were both taken to the administration building for interrogation by prison officials, FBI agents, and state investigators. They wanted to know the details of how we escaped and who had helped us.

Malcolm was taken into one room and I was taken to another. Apparently, he agreed to answer questions, because they talked with him for quite some time.

When my interrogation started, I just repeated, "I have nothing to say." After a few repetitions, I was unceremoniously loaded into a prison car for the drive to the maximum-security unit. As we approached the well-lit compound, with its high, barbed fence and foreboding guard towers, I knew that this dismal place was going to be my home for a long time. The electric gate slowly opened, and we drove into the compound. The guards took me into the building and untied my hands. The heavy steel door clanged shut behind me with a solemn, final *thud*.

I felt as if I had been sealed in a tomb.

I had to strip naked once again and allow the prison guards to thoroughly examine me for contraband. They gave me fresh underwear, then escorted me to the cellblock and my new cell. I would spend the next three years of my life in a six-by-nine-foot space.

Since my last stay in maximum security, the number of inmates being held for "safekeeping" had increased considerably and now consisted of an entire cellblock.

Conditions were similar to those in death row. We were locked in our cells all the time except for two showers a week. We ate two meals a day in our cell, were allowed to buy snacks, and could have radios, books, and magazines. The biggest difference was the noise. Death row was mostly quiet and subdued. In safekeeping, noise was nearly incessant, incoherent, and frankly, nerve-racking. Some prisoners would shout from one end of the cellblock to the other to talk. Others would blast their radios.

On one occasion, several inmates retaliated against the noise of others and began a "noise war" that lasted for a couple of days. Because this war affected everyone, even quiet prisoners became involved in the back-and-forth. Some would loudly rattle their cell doors. Others would turn up the volume on their radios. Still others would shout or scream. In various ways, different ones would periodically make loud noises to assure that no one could sleep. At last, probably because of fatigue, they called a truce. Loud talk and loud radios continued on a sporadic basis throughout my stay in that cellblock.

Noise was not the only problem. Mississippi summers are hot and humid. We had no air conditioning, only a ventilator fan. Although the fan was better than nothing, it only produced a slow, tortuous movement of the hot air. As the temperature rose during the day, the cells heated up like an oven until late at night. Often it was so hot that I couldn't get to sleep before 10:00 or 11:00 p.m.

Among the prisoners housed at the maximum-security unit at this time were several members of a black revolutionary group called the Republic of New Africa (RNA). Their organization was seeking to establish a separate nation for blacks within the United States (especially the Southeastern United States) and to obtain reparations from the U.S. government for the legacy of slavery. The RNA's "Provisional Government" had established a headquarters in Jackson, which led to a violent confrontation with police and FBI agents. I had several conversations with one of their leaders and found him to be an interesting person.

As I listened to him describe what he believed and what he was trying to do, it struck me that his path to radicalization was not too different from mine.

After analyzing the security system in safekeeping, I had concluded that escape was not possible. As the weeks turned into months, in order to keep my sanity, I read. And read. And read. Books were my relief from the oppressive boredom of prison life, but the material I was reading kept pouring more and more hateful ideas into my mind.

Some of the key books that had influenced me in the past were *The Protocols of the Learned Elders of Zion* (author anonymous) and *The International Jew* by Henry Ford. But now I moved on to other works, such as *The Inequality of the Human Races* by Count Arthur de Gobineau, *White America* by Earnest Sevier Cox, *Imperium* by Ulick Varange (Francis Parker Yockey), *Mein Kampf* by Adolf Hitler, *The Importance of Race in Civilization* by Wayne MacLeod, and *Atlas Shrugged* by Ayn Rand. I also read the *American Mercury* magazine, the *Thunderbolt* newspaper (published by the NSRP), the *Fiery Cross* magazine (published by the United Klans of America), and *American Opinion* magazine (published by the John Birch Society). I was able to order most of these by mail. Fortunately, none of the other inmates knew what I was reading, so I had no problems. The guards, of course, knew, but they didn't seem to care.

Reading this type of material served only to reinforce my views about the Jews, the supremacy of the white race, and the inferiority of black people. Instead of being rehabilitated, I was diving even deeper into the darkness. I had not yet learned the first law of holes: when you are in one, stop digging.

During this period, my parents continued to make the long trip from Mobile every two weeks to see me. Sometimes my sister and brother also came. Since I was in maximum security again, they could stay only for two hours, but I always felt encouraged after seeing them. Unfortunately,

I was still so self-centered that I had little awareness of or consideration for their feelings or needs. I was generally moody, frustrated, and irritable, which was symptomatic of my depression. I sometimes would flare up at them about inconsequential things. No doubt the long, weary ride home gave them no encouragement, only grief. But they loved me and were committed to helping me as best they could. How they did it, I cannot fathom. My mother, in particular, continued to pray for me and to hope in God for a good outcome eventually. She wrote letters to the governor and to the prison superintendent on my behalf, seeking to ensure good treatment. In spite of many reasons to give up, she persevered in hope and never lost faith in God. Like Monica, the mother of Augustine, to whom Saint Ambrose said, "It cannot be that the son of those tears should perish," my mother shed many tears over many years.[1] And as it was for Augustine, and so many after him, so would it soon be for me.

# 13
# ENCOUNTER WITH TRUTH AND LIGHT

After about six months of confinement on the safekeeping cellblock, I was moved to death row. This largely resulted from my parents' requests for a less noisy place for me to live. Death row was far quieter and better suited for prolonged incarceration. However, life was still miserable, and my prospects for the future were worse than ever.

I was locked in a tiny cell by myself twenty-four hours a day, with no recreation or exercise. Other than two showers a week that took fewer than fifteen minutes each, I stayed in that cell. A guard brought meals that were passed in through an opening in the bars. Words like *drab*, *dismal*, and *depressing* cannot begin to describe the severe loneliness of my situation. The seeming hopelessness of my predicament was reinforced when prison officials told me that FBI director J. Edgar Hoover and Mississippi governor John Bell Williams had both stressed that I should never be released from my cell. I was stuck with myself and my thoughts, and I could see no way out. Life seemed hopeless.

My thinking and feelings spiraled downward even further.

Kathy Ainsworth's death in the Meridian ambush had grieved me from the beginning, but now it weighed on me even more heavily. It was heartrending. My decision to take her on the Meridian bombing, though she was willing, cost her life. Likewise, my recruiting of Louis Shadoan ultimately cost his life. My hand in the cause of these two deaths weighed heavy on me. My depression intensified, worse than ever. It felt as though a dark cloud would sometimes descend on me, causing me to lose all perspective. Life seemed hopeless and not worth living. As before in the Lauderdale County Jail, I began again to think about how I could kill myself to escape the misery.

This time I would make sure it worked. I saved up a handful of sleeping pills prescribed for me by the prison doctor and took them all at once. These, I thought, would certainly be fatal. I was fully expecting to die and wake up in heaven. But a guard on the night shift made a rare, unscheduled patrol through the cellblock and saw me staggering around my cell, incoherent. He called the prison doctor, who came immediately and administered emergency treatment, saving my life. I have no memory of the event. I regained consciousness only to face once again the unpleasant reality I was trying to escape.

With nothing else to do, I resumed my reading. But this time, instead of reading hateful material, I moved in a different direction. The book *Imperium* contained a lot of neofascist philosophy, but it also quoted some noted philosophers. Rather than stop at the author's take on the great philosophers, some of whom intrigued me and stimulated my thinking, I decided to read them for myself.

I began with G. W. F. Hegel's *Philosophy of History*, which was beyond me at points but not without value, as it gave me an understanding of the dialectical view of history that was central to Marxist thinking. Then I read Oswald Spengler's *The Decline of the West*, which was also beyond me at points, but again, not without value. It introduced me to the idea that cultures have a life cycle—they are born, grow to maturity, and then decline and die.

I needed something more foundational and soon moved to the ancient writings of Plato, Aristotle, and the Stoics. I was fascinated by Plato's reasoning and his thinking on the immortality of the soul and the ideal state; the objectivity of truth, goodness, and beauty; and the implications for a disinterested pursuit of truth. Socrates's idea that an unexamined life is not worth living also resonated strongly with me. I was beginning to see that I had not really done any serious thinking for myself, or any examination of my life, but had simply accepted ideas that sounded plausible to me.

Most important, Plato and the Stoics helped me recognize and reflect on how transitory life really is. Thus, the pursuit of truth for our brief life in this world took on even greater importance to me. I decided that I would search for truth, regardless of where this journey took me and what truth turned out to be. Up to this point, I had read only those books that were consistent with my ideological bias. I had avoided books, writings, and ideas that were opposed to my views or that were incongruent in any way. I dismissed such material as worthless. I never imagined that opposing views might contain at least some elements of truth that would make sense to me.

Unknowingly, I was experiencing an intellectual awakening that would eventually liberate my mind and prepare my heart for a spiritual awakening. Much of this intellectual awakening came through books I had purchased by mail from the Conservative Book Club, which I had recently discovered.

One of the first was *Legacy of Freedom*, a book on political philosophy by George C. Roche. Many passages spoke to me, but I was powerfully struck by these particular words: "A man willing to judge 'truth' on its merits is the true realist because he is able to understand that the structure of reality is independent of his own desires. He grasps the fact that the world was created before he arrived and will still be here when he, in his earthly form, has departed."[1]

This thought reinforced my desire for truth and triggered a profound change in me. I saw even more clearly that I must seek truth regardless of what it might entail: if I should find error in views that I had so zealously cherished, then I would have to abandon them—no matter how important they might be to me.

Because of this newfound desire for truth, my intellect was now guiding me with a new goal of rigorous objectivity. My undeveloped critical thinking skills began to grow. And even though complete objectivity was impossible, my commitment to this new way of seeing would soon spell the end of my radical ideology and the other forms of deception that had bound me for years.

As I continued to read *Legacy of Freedom*, I came to understand that the events of history were inextricably bound up with, and reflective of, a highly complex matrix of political, social, cultural, economic, religious, and philosophical currents—all of which interacted with one another. Wars and revolutions were not simply part of "Jewish conspiracies," nor was Communism simply a "Jewish plot."

About this time, the book *Suicide of the West* by James Burnham came into my hands. I had seen it advertised, and the title intrigued me, especially in light of my reading of Oswald Spengler, so I ordered it. Burnham was a brilliant intellectual and professor of philosophy at New York University. Among other things, he was particularly helpful to me in exposing the fallacies of anti-Semitic ideology, which I had swallowed hook, line, and sinker, with no investigation or analysis.

The lights came on for me when I read these words:

A convinced believer in the anti-Semitic ideology tells me that the Bolshevik revolution is a Jewish plot. I point out to him that the revolution was led to its first major victory by a non-Jew, Lenin. He then explains that Lenin was the pawn of Trotsky, Radek, Kamenev, and Zinoviev and other Jews who were in the Bolshevik High Command. I remind him that Lenin's successor as leader of the revolution, the non-Jew Stalin, killed off all those Jews; and that Stalin has been followed by the non-Jew, Khrushchev, under whose rule there have been notable revivals of anti-Semitic attitudes and conduct. He then informs me that the seeming Soviet anti-Semitism is only a fraud invented by the Jewish press, and that Stalin and Khrushchev are really Jews whose names have been changed with a total substitution of forged records. Suppose I am able to present documents that even he will have to admit show this to be impossible. He is still unmoved. He tells me that the real Jewish center that controls the revolution and the entire world conspiracy is not in Russia anyway, but in Antwerp, Tel Aviv, Lhasa, New York, or somewhere, and that it has deliberately eliminated the Jews from the public officialdom of the Bolshevik countries in order to conceal its hand and deceive the world about what is going on.[2]

Burnham helped me recognize a significant danger, one to which I had fallen prey: becoming an ideologue. As Burnham explained,

An ideologue—one who thinks ideologically—can't lose. He can't lose because his answer, his interpretation and his attitudes have been determined in advance of the particular experience or observation. His thoughts are derived from the ideology and are not subject to the facts. There is no possible argument, observation or experiment that could disprove a firm ideological belief for the very simple reason that an ideologue will not accept any argument, observation, or experiment as constituting disproof.[3]

This described me and the ideological thinking which lay beneath my anti-Semitism and racism. Once I realized this, the foundations of the Cause began to crumble. My eyes were opened to see that the historical facts simply did not support the idea of a Jewish conspiracy. As for blacks and the civil rights movement, Burnham deftly demolished racist arguments as well:

> I mention after hearing him assert the innate inferiority of the Negro race, the fact that in baseball, boxing, track and field sports, Negroes are the champions. These purely physical achievements, he explains, are proof of how close Negroes remain to animals in the evolutionary scale. I add the names of Negro musicians, singers, actors and writers of the first rank. Naturally, he comments, they carry over a sense of rhythm from the tribal dance and tom-tom ceremonies. I ask how many law graduates of his state university could stand up against Judge Thurgood Marshall; how many sociologists against Professor C. Eric Lincoln; how many psychologists against Professor Kenneth Clark? Doubtless all such have plenty of white blood, he answers, but in any case they are only exceptions to prove the general rule of inferiority; that is confirmed by the low intellectual attainments of the average Negro. I observe that the average Negro has been educated in worse schools, and for fewer years, than the average white. Of course, he agrees: No use wasting good education on low-grade material.[4]

Recognizing the intellectual, philosophical, and moral bankruptcy of far-right ideology initiated a process of liberation in my life. I had been trapped in an ideological prison that dulled my thinking and feeling. But now roots of that ideology were being severed, and the prison door was opening. I had been driven by fears that were rooted in malicious lies that had produced anger, hatred, and all that follows in their wake. My mind was becoming free to think clearly, and I started to feel a deep desire for truth. No longer did I have to be careful of what I read lest some "Jewish propaganda" inadvertently poison my thinking. No longer did I have to rationalize away inconvenient truths and realities that did not fit into my ideology. I was now free to read and study anything I desired and to judge it according to its own merits. Correspondence with reality had become my criterion of truth. And truth had become my goal. I would later learn that the pursuit of truth for its own sake was a vital part of escaping ideological captivity.

Several months into this journey, I came to the Bible. Or rather, I came back to it. I felt an especially strong desire to read the Gospels in the New Testament. I can't really say why, other than on the human level, it was to some extent part of my search for truth. It did not arise out of a search for solace, or escape, or a way to get out of the trouble I was in. Nor was it from a concern to improve my relationship with God, which I thought was fine. Like my comrades in the Cause, I had seen myself as fighting for God and country. God was on our side. We were true patriots. The Communists, Jews, liberals, the civil rights movement, and the corrupt federal government were the enemy. They were working together to actively undermine the Christian beliefs and values that our nation had been founded on. We saw our resistance as completely justified for preserving white, Christian America—desperate times required desperate measures. The end justified the means. While we knew what we were doing was illegal, we never entertained the thought that it might be sinful or evil. That kind of thinking had now crumbled, but I had not yet seen how distorted my ideas about God were. Reading the Gospels was about to change that, as it has for many people down through history.

As I began to read, in the New Testament this time, it was unlike my previous experiences. When I turned the pages, it was like the lights in a darkened theater being slowly turned up. Now I began to see, as it were, first the dim outlines of things, then colors, then textures. I was able to understand what I read in a way I never had before. The words on the pages seemed to be speaking directly to me. As I read the Gospels each day for a couple of weeks or so, the light became brighter and brighter, and my spiritual sight got clearer and clearer. One truth after another was registering with me. It was if I had been blind all my life and had just received my sight!

For the first time, I realized on a deeply personal level that I had sinned against God and needed his forgiveness. My sins were becoming clearer to me: anger, hatred, and violence toward my enemies; using people for my own selfish ends, especially Kathy Ainsworth and Louis Shadoan, and their resulting deaths; lying, stealing, sexual immorality, and more. And then there was the impact of my sins on my family and those who loved me—the anguish they had suffered and the shame and stigma of being related to me.

It was becoming clear that my Christianity had been an empty sham. I had been a Christian in name only. I had given a mental assent to Christianity to the extent that I acknowledged the right truths and said the right words when I had been baptized. But I had never thought of myself as a particularly bad person or felt the weight of my sins, and I continued in them with no hesitation, sense of guilt, or desire to be delivered. In short, I had never come to genuine repentance, which along with faith, is essential to being born again.

Like a laser beam, one Bible verse struck my heart with conviction more powerfully than any other: "For what will it profit a man if he gains the whole world and forfeits his soul? Or what shall a man give in return for his soul?" (Matthew 16:26). For the past five years, I had been selling my soul to gain the part of the world that was important to me. My commitment to the Cause, which was very real, was at a deeper level rooted in selfish ambition—trying to satisfy my ego and advance my position in the far-right movement. Gaining recognition and respect from my friends had been my top priority. How I wished that I could go back in time and take a different path in life from the one I had taken!

As the full impact of all this began to break in on me, I was overcome with deep sorrow for all the prejudice, hatred, violence, immorality, and much more—for the evil of my whole life. I had been living for myself as far back as I could remember—what pleased me, made me feel good, and made me look good were what guided me. And now I was reaping what I had sown. Specific sins came to my mind one after another, as person after person and event after event rose up against me. How could I have done these things? As I saw what I was really like, I wept and wept and wept.

In the midst of this, words that I had learned in my childhood, words that had not helped me earlier, now helped me know where to turn: "For God so loved the world, that he gave his only Son, that whoever believes in him should not perish but have eternal life. For God did not send his Son into the world to condemn the world, but in order that the world might be saved through him" (John 3:16–17).

Finally, in the quiet of a summer night in 1970, I got on my knees on the concrete floor of my cell and prayed a simple prayer: *Lord Jesus Christ, I have ruined my life and the lives of others and committed many sins. Please forgive me, take over my life, and do whatever you want with me.* I gave myself to Jesus as fully as I knew how. When I knelt, I had no idea whether he would want the wreck that was my life. But thanks be to God, he did!

In that moment I felt as if a thousand pounds had been lifted off my shoulders. Something deep within me had changed—new life had invaded my heart. There was no high drama or frothy excitement, only a sense, an inner knowing, that Jesus had heard my prayer and I was now somehow different than I had been before I prayed.

More than two hundred years earlier, Charles Wesley described well what I experienced in that cell:

> Long my imprisoned spirit lay,
> Fast bound in sin and nature's night;
> Thine eye diffused a quickening ray—
> I woke, the dungeon flamed with light;
> My chains fell off, my heart was free,
> I rose, went forth, and followed Thee.[5]

# NEW LIFE!

T he apostle Paul said "if anyone is in Christ, he is a new creation" (2
Cor. 5:17). Through trusting in Jesus Christ, that is what had happened to me. It was very different from the profession of faith I had made
in my early teens, which had no impact on me. And it was not a matter
of swapping ideology for religion or simply turning over a new leaf. No,
Christ had first led me out of error into truth, then out of darkness into
light, and finally out of death into life. I was now spiritually alive, and
God was real to me in a way I had never known before. Even though I was
locked in a six-by-nine-foot cell twenty-four hours a day, I had a freedom
in my mind and heart that made it bearable. Gone was the hopelessness, and joy had come in its place. The words of John Newton rang true,
"Amazing grace, how sweet the sound, that saved a wretch like me. I once
was lost but now am found, was blind, but now I see."[1]

I experienced a number of immediate and dramatic changes in my
life. One of the most noticeable differences was my language—I used to

curse with every other breath. But the morning after I came to Christ, the profanity disappeared and has never been a problem since. Why I experienced such a quick deliverance from this particular sin is a mystery, but I took it as evidence of God's power at work in my life. Perhaps it was also meant to be an encouragement from God that he would deliver me from other, more difficult sins that would need to be dealt with in the future.

I wish all my sins had gone away as quickly as this one, but that is not how the Christian life works. I didn't realize at that point just how deep and pervasive sin was in my life, or how long the journey of transformation would be. Choice by choice, I had corrupted my soul over the years and made my life a terrible mess. My twisted beliefs were a mess, my damaged emotional life was a mess, and my corrupted will was a mess. God's transformation process would take time. And it would not be complete in this life, but as theologian and philosopher Francis Schaeffer observed, if we cooperate with God, it will produce "substantial healing."[2] Jesus alluded to this when he said, "If you abide in my word, you are truly my disciples, and you will know the truth, and the truth will set you free" (John 8:31–32).

I immediately began daily Bible reading and prayer. My appetite for Scripture was voracious. I read for hours every day. I focused on the New Testament at first, but soon I was reading the Old Testament as well. It was all so fresh, so new. I was exploring a new world, and it was exciting. Every day I discovered more about who God was, what he had done in the past, what he would do in the future, and how he wanted me to live today. Prayer began to flow freely. Before this, I had occasionally said a Puritan bedtime prayer that my mother taught me in childhood: "Now I lay me down to sleep; I pray the Lord my soul to keep. If I die before I wake, I pray the Lord my soul to take. Amen." Other than that, the only other times I remember praying earnestly were a couple of times when I was in a real jam. But now prayer seemed natural and became a daily experience, first thing in the morning.

In addition, with guidance from the chaplain, I was now spending hours each day exploring theology, apologetics, and related disciplines of study. I had what Anselm described as "faith seeking understanding."[3] A whole new world had been opened up to me, and it was thrilling to explore. I was on a great adventure of discovery that was both exciting and satisfying even in the midst of my confinement.

But the most profound change was how I viewed my old life. I wanted no part of my previous, evil life; I only wanted to leave it behind. There was no way to go back and undo the sins of my past, but there was a way to go forward and live a very different life. I now wanted to live for God. I wanted to draw near to him and to follow Jesus. I didn't know how to do this, but the enlightenment and encouragement I received from reading the Bible fed and intensified this desire and gave me direction.

The apostle Paul wrote, "Do not conform to the pattern of this world, but be transformed by the renewing of your mind" (Romans 12:2 NIV). Though I didn't realize it at the time, by immersing myself in Scripture, I was exposing myself to the Holy Spirit's renewing influences in my mind. This renewal began to change my view of God and people and how to live.

I took encouragement from the stories of the Old Testament and the accounts of Jesus and the apostles in the New Testament, as I saw how God had worked in the lives of his people down through the centuries. King Manasseh of Judah, for example, was one of the most evil people in the Bible, yet through God's severe chastisement he came to repentance, and God ultimately had mercy on him and used him to undo at least some of the evil he had caused.[4] Saul of Tarsus, a religious zealot filled with anger and hatred, severely persecuted the followers of Jesus, yet Jesus saved him, transformed him into the apostle Paul, and used him to do much good over the rest of his life.[5] These stories gave encouragement that, like them, maybe God had some purpose for my life. Maybe I could serve God in some way and do good the rest of my life.

The fact that I should have been dead was not lost on me. During the Meridian ambush a hail of bullets—some even fired at point-blank range—had filled the air around me, yet none had proved lethal. I had been hit four times at close range with double-aught buckshot and lived, while Kathy Ainsworth had been hit by a single shot while sitting right next to me, and she died.

What's more, none of the shots I fired that night were lethal either. I'd shot Officer Mike Hatcher in the heart, and miraculously he had lived. Had he died, I would certainly have been given a death sentence and executed. The thought was chilling.

And then there was the prison break. In another barrage of gunfire that killed my fellow escapee, Louis Shadoan, I emerged unscathed. Minutes earlier I had been standing right where he was and would have been the one who died had he not relieved me early.

I could only conclude that my survival was God's doing. It was inexplicable on any other grounds. If that was true—and to me it was logically inescapable—then God must have some purpose for my life. This gave me a glimmer of hope that a better future was ahead, not just in the world to come but here on earth as well.

I was only at the beginning, but by his grace I was on the way. John Newton described me when he said, "I am not what I ought to be. I am not what I want to be. I am not what I hope to be. But still, I am not what I used to be. And by the grace of God, I am what I am."[6]

I know that some people feel their sins are so bad that they cannot be forgiven, and they have a hard time accepting God's forgiveness. But that was not a big problem for me. God's love and forgiveness were so clearly undeserved, yet so life-giving and liberating, that they eclipsed everything else. Knowing that God loved me, had spared my life, and saved me brought joy to my heart. The Bible says, "If we confess our sins, he is faithful and just to forgive us our sins and to cleanse us from all unrighteousness" (1 John 1:9). Those words were a healing balm to my heart and soul.

I found it easy to accept God's forgiveness, but it took some time to realize that I in turn needed to forgive others. And there were definitely people I needed to forgive. The police and the Roberts brothers, who had betrayed me to the FBI, were at the top of the list. I hated them. As I continued to read the Bible daily, I discovered that hating people was a serious sin, and that forgiving people was a nonnegotiable requirement from God's point of view. In the Lord's Prayer, Jesus taught that we should ask God to "forgive us our debts, as we also have forgiven our debtors" (Matthew 6:12), thereby connecting God's forgiveness of our sins against him with our forgiveness of others' sins against us. Then, to make sure no one could miss the point, at the end of the Lord's Prayer, he said, "For if you forgive others their trespasses, your heavenly Father will also forgive you, but if you do not forgive others their trespasses, neither will your Father forgive your trespasses" (6:14–15).

If I was serious about following Jesus, I had to forgive those against whom I had grudges, something I'd not even considered before. By an act of my will, I chose to forgive the police officers who killed Kathy. I also forgave the ones who shot me when I was lying faceup, unarmed, and barely conscious on the ground. They had tried their best to kill me, even though I was not a threat to them. Although I realized that I deserved what I got, I had nevertheless been angry and bitter toward these men.

While more difficult, I even forgave the Roberts brothers, who had set me up and betrayed me for selfish gain. I had looked at them as traitors and scum of the earth. I hated them and thought they deserved to die. But when I looked honestly at my own responsibility in what happened and realized that I was no better than them, it gave me a different perspective. By God's grace, I chose to forgive them as well.

I was discovering that "if the Son sets you free, you will be free indeed" (John 8:36).

I was free indeed.

\*    \*    \*

Aleksandr Solzhenitsyn wrote, "Gradually, it was disclosed to me that the line separating good and evil passes not through states, nor between classes, nor between political parties either—but right through every human heart—and through all human hearts."[7] This insight also came to me, and I recognized that it had been easy to label others as evil and think I was one of the good guys. Now I saw that I had been far worse than those I had hated. They had been risking their lives to pursue freedom and justice; I had been risking mine for hatred and oppression.

One day I read, "If anyone says, 'I love God,' and hates his brother, he is a liar; for he who does not love his brother whom he has seen cannot love God whom he has not seen. And this commandment we have from him: whoever loves God must also love his brother" (1 John 4:20–21). When I read this passage, I knew God was speaking to me about my attitude toward black people. Just before my conversion, I had seen the errors of racist thinking and realized my hatred was ultimately based on lies and distortions. But there was a great difference between not hating people and actually loving and accepting them. God was now dealing with my heart at a deeper level. God was calling me to love black people, and not just those who were believers. Once I saw this, my heart quickly changed. The way I looked at the black inmates on the cellblock changed, and once I was released into the general prison population, friendships developed.

As strange as it may seem, my hatred for Jewish people had also vanished even though it had been the strongest of all. It had been based on anti-Semitic lies and propaganda that I discovered were false even before coming to Christ. Those lies had fueled anger, then hatred. But when that house of cards collapsed, my hatred of the Jews evaporated as well. The truth was that Jewish people had never done anything to me. I had hated them without cause.

Hatred of the Communists was last to go. I had always justified hating them because they were enemies of America who had done horrific evil on a vast scale under the Soviets and Maoists (estimated at 60–100 million deaths).[8] And through their atheism and persecution of Christians, they were also enemies of God. But I came to see that I could not hate them either. They needed Christ as much as anyone else.

To love God and to follow Jesus meant to reject hatred toward anyone. Instead, I was to love my neighbor and even my enemies. And soon, God would bring black and Jewish people into my life in a more personal way, giving me the opportunity to do so.

Hatred had been a spiritual cancer in my soul. And it had grown and metastasized throughout my entire belief system. But God had given me a regimen of divine surgery and chemotherapy to get rid of it and had planted love in my heart in its place. Of course, many people were slow to believe that someone like me could be set free from such intense hatred, especially so quickly. In the normal course of human affairs, that just doesn't happen. But when the Holy Spirit is at work, the impossible becomes possible.

Racial and ethnic hatred was only one area of my life that needed change. Though I didn't realize it at the time, I was at the beginning of a process that would touch all areas of my life over time. It is worth mentioning some of the other ways God was working at this stage.

One of the prison chaplains, Rev. Glenn Howell, played a vital role in my life during this formative period. A recent graduate of Asbury Theological Seminary in Kentucky, he had just joined the prison staff as a chaplain. One day Chaplain Selby McManus, the head chaplain, brought him to the maximum-security unit. He stopped in front of my cell to talk through the bars. In his late twenties, Glenn was a solidly built guy with a thick head of hair, a ready smile, and an easy manner. He seemed like a man of God, and I enjoyed meeting him.

Although he had a strong desire to help inmates, Glenn was not naive or gullible and could read people well. That was important in prison ministry. Some inmates turn to religion as a way to gain certain benefits in prison. They are con men who are trying to manipulate the system. Others turn to religion as a crutch, hoping it will support them in a hard situation in life. Once they're released, their religion often falls away. But in some cases, people really do come to saving faith in Jesus, begin to change while in prison, and continue to follow him after they get out. Glenn seemed to think that I might have had a true conversion and was willing to help where he could in the process.

I was eager to read anything dealing with biblical faith, and I asked if he had any books I might read. One of the books he gave me was *Christianity Rightly So Called* by Samuel G. Craig—a clear explanation of the basics of biblical faith. This gave me an invaluable orientation to foundational biblical beliefs. Through the footnote citations in that book, I became aware of other good books and was soon ordering them by mail. And through those books, I discovered others. I soon got *Systematic Theology* by Louis Berkhof, which I loved. *Mere Christianity, Miracles, The Problem of Pain, God in the Dock*, and other books by C. S. Lewis followed.

While all of this reading was helpful in understanding my new faith, I also really needed practical instruction on how to live the Christian life—how to grow in grace and follow Jesus in daily life. This season of intense but informal theological study in my cell lasted about two years. It was a time of significant intellectual growth for me. Through it, I was beginning to see what C. S. Lewis meant when he said, "I believe in Christianity as I believe the sun has risen. Not only because I see it, but because by it I see everything else."[9] But ironically, after a good start, I experienced a time of increasing spiritual "dryness." I would later learn that this is not uncommon for those who love ideas and knowledge and overdevelop their intellectual life to the neglect of their spiritual life. My focus on acquiring theological knowledge was overshadowing my daily, personal fellowship with God. Without the freshness of regular communion with God, I had become spiritually stale and arid. Knowing about God and actually knowing God in a personal and intimate way are two very different things. It would take years for me to learn that "the longest journey in life is the eighteen inches between your head and your heart."[10]

Another reason for my dryness was the growth of pride in the knowledge I had been acquiring. The Bible strongly warns against the great danger of pride and says, "For though the LORD is high, he regards the lowly, but the haughty he knows from afar" (Psalm 138:6). As Thomas à Kempis said so profoundly, "God walks with the simple; He reveals himself to the lowly; He discloses His meaning to pure minds, and hides His grace from the curious and the proud."[11] That was another truth that would also take me years to learn.

My spiritual growth was hindered in other ways—major ones that I could do nothing about. I needed a church—fellowship and prayer with other believers and an opportunity to regularly worship God and take Communion. I also needed personal discipling—spiritual mentoring by a mature believer who knew the Bible well, understood the process of spiritual growth, and could spend the time needed to guide me. However, my confinement to a cell twenty-four hours a day under maximum-security conditions made all those things impossible. Without access to most of the essential means of spiritual growth, my development was significantly impeded.

\*     \*     \*

Not long after I came to Christ, and filled with the zeal of a new convert, I wrote letters to the people I'd been involved with in the Ku Klux Klan, telling them how wrong we had all been to think that we could hate black people and Jews and still be Christians. How could we think we were true followers of Jesus if we hated other people? I hoped they would see their error and find true salvation as I had, and I prayed for them.

Unfortunately, they did not see it that way. Instead, as I would later discover, they started looking for ways to have me killed in prison.

# NEW FRIENDS

One day in early 1971, I had a surprising visitor. The guard announced that Reverend Kenneth Dean of Jackson, head of the Mississippi Council on Human Relations, was waiting to see me. Reverend Dean was a prominent civil rights advocate who had been interested in my case from the beginning. Based on what he had seen and heard, he felt that I had been the victim of illegal entrapment by the FBI. He had driven up to Parchman to talk to me about it. He and his wife, Mary, had already sought out and befriended my parents.

Ken was a complicated person with whom I disagreed on politics and theology. Yet he was genuinely concerned about my welfare. He saw racists as people he was called to love. Over the years he befriended not only me but Sam Bowers and other Klan leaders as well. He won them over with the same unassuming sincerity with which he had won me over. As you might imagine, this made him an enigma to people on all sides. I had assumed that all liberal civil rights activists would naturally hate Southern racists.

But that was not true of Ken, nor, as I would soon discover, of several others I would meet. I had also assumed that it was impossible for a conservative to be friends with a liberal without compromising in some way. But I found that that was not true either. I discovered that it is possible for people to hold very different views on important issues yet not be enemies. In parting, Ken gave me a gift: *Pensées* by Blaise Pascal, whose wisdom I still find inspiring. Though neither of us could have anticipated it at the time, Ken would eventually play an important role in my being released from prison.

About this time, another relationship began developing with an equally unlikely person. Joyce Watts, the wife of FBI agent Frank Watts (who had interrogated me when I was awaiting trial in Meridian), wrote me a letter and sent some Christian books. Joyce had been impacted by the charismatic movement and explained that she had been praying for me regularly since my arrest in 1968. In fact, her whole women's prayer group in Meridian, Mississippi, had prayed for me weekly for about two years. They believed that God could still do miracles and were asking him to do a big one by saving me and transforming my life. During those two years, their prayers would have made no sense to me at all, but now it was clear that these faithful intercessors—along with my mother and others—had indeed helped pray me into the kingdom of God.

After word got out that I'd experienced a religious conversion, Frank Watts and his partner, Jack Rucker, came to see me on the orders of FBI director J. Edgar Hoover, who thought I was trying to use religion as a ruse to gain another opportunity to escape. He sent my former interrogators on an official visit to assess the situation.

Frank and Jack talked with me for a while, trying to understand what was going on with me. I shared openly how my eyes had been opened and I had come to true faith in Christ. They listened with intense interest because, as Frank later told me, he had never seen such a change in a person. He said even my countenance was different. And then they asked me an extremely tough question: "Now that you really know Jesus Christ, don't you think it is your duty to testify against your associates and put them behind bars? After all, they are dangerous people and have broken the laws. For the good of society, they need to be locked up."

I was still very immature in my faith at this point, especially in the practical application of my faith to daily life. My response probably seemed like a cop-out to them. However, I had been deeply influenced by years of watching war movies (where a prisoner gave only name, rank, and serial number when captured) and by the Klan's code of secrecy.

As I explained to them, the crimes I committed were done out of a common commitment to a cause and mutual trust. It would be wrong, I reasoned, to testify against my cohorts now—especially since they were no longer engaged in violence. Most of them had already been charged with other crimes. The likelihood of their doing anything else was very small. If I testified against them, so my reasoning went, my newfound relationship with Christ would appear to be just a con game to gain an early release from prison by becoming "righteous." That, it seemed to me, would dishonor the Lord. However, I did promise that if any of them were suspected to be planning violence again, I would let them know that if they went through with it, I would testify against them.

Frank later told me that the changes he saw in me that day caused him to reexamine his own life. Although he was a good, moral man, a church member, and considered himself a Christian, he came to see that he had never really had a personal relationship with Christ. The recognition that he had had only an outward form of religion led him to a very real, life-changing and personal faith in Jesus that would steadily mature over the years. After that, Frank Watts and I became good friends. Neither of us had any idea at the time what a vital role Frank would play in my life in the future.

\*     \*     \*

I had been in the maximum-security unit for two years when Sergeant E. R. Moody, who was in charge of the unit, came to my cell one day and asked, "How would you like to get out of your cell for a few hours a day to do clerical work for me in the office?" I was floored by his question. He said, "This could be an opportunity to prove yourself, and it might eventually get you out of maximum security and into the general prison population." He also explained that he had gained a lot of respect for my parents, especially my mother, during their visits. He had also watched me during the year or so since I had come to the Lord and had seen the changes in my life. He had decided to help me if he could. And so I worked for Sergeant Moody a full year, doing the best job I possibly could.

Much later, I learned that Sergeant Moody had gone to the superintendent and put his job on the line to get permission to offer me this job. There was no reason for him or anyone else to take such an initiative on my behalf. But for some reason, he did.

Now that I was out of my cell each day, I had more opportunities to help others. Ironically, the first person I helped to grow spiritually was someone I would have never even spoken to before—a young black man named Gary who was a cook in maximum security. A common plight (prison) and a shared interest in the Lord drew us together as friends, and he began to ask me questions about things he was reading in the Bible. I was only one or two steps ahead of Gary, but I was able to answer some of his questions. Although I knew nothing about helping others grow in their faith at the time, this was my first experience of something I would be doing for the rest of my life—trying to help people grow as disciples of Jesus.

\*　　\*　　\*

The year 1972 brought several dramatic changes in my prison status. The new governor, Bill Waller, had taken office in January. In February, he appointed John Collier, a prominent plantation owner from the

Mississippi Delta and a dedicated Christian layman, as superintendent of the state penitentiary. One day that spring, Mr. Collier was making an inspection tour of the maximum-security unit and noticed my cell—cluttered as it was with stacks of Christian books and literature. He wanted to know who was assigned there. After completing his inspection, he came into the office where I worked and saw even more faith-related books stacked around my work space.

Superintendent Collier introduced himself to me and asked if the books were mine. I stood up and answered yes. He asked me, "Do you know the Lord?" "Yes, sir," I replied. He said that he did, too, and after a brief conversation, he left. This seemingly chance encounter was far more significant than I knew. During the next couple of months, I saw Mr. Collier two or three times, and then only briefly. But some of his key staff—the prison chief of security, the staff psychologist, and the four chaplains, who visited maximum security often—had gotten to know me well. This would soon bring surprising developments.

In May, my friend and mentor, Sergeant Moody, retired. My new supervisor, Sergeant Patrick Mooney, who also worked in maximum security, recommended me for trusty status. This meant I would be given more freedom within the prison. Much to my surprise, the prison classification committee, with the support of the chaplains and the prison psychologist, unanimously approved the recommendation, and Superintendent Collier concurred. Three years after my escape and recapture, I was given a status of trust and responsibility that no one could have predicted and some of the security personnel thought was crazy. They assumed my conversion was "jailhouse religion"—the temporary adoption of religion as a psychological coping mechanism or as a pretense to gain some advantage while in confinement.

My first time out of the maximum-security unit as a trusty was with Chaplain Glenn Howell, who took the risk of inviting me to his home for dinner and fellowship with his wife and children. Mary was a great cook and a warm, loving person. She treated me to the best meal I'd had in four years. What a gift to be in normal surroundings, eating and talking with ordinary people, with little children running around. It was the first of a number of such occasions with Glenn and his family that I would enjoy in the years ahead.

Shortly after that, my supervisors felt that the time had come for me to be released from the maximum-security unit altogether. I was assigned to work as a clerk in the chaplain's office, in the administration building. My new living quarters was a garage apartment in back of the superintendent's home, where the Collier family lived.

For someone with a record like mine and just out of maximum security, this kind of move was more than unusual or even extraordinary—it was unheard-of. Skeptics on the prison staff thought Mr. Collier was naive, if not stupid, and that I had conned him with my "jailhouse religion." They predicted I would escape again, as there were no guards and no locked doors to prevent my leaving either the administration building or my garage apartment.

I could have easily walked away at night and no one would have known for eight hours. But escaping never entered my mind. God had changed my heart. I knew that his plan for my life did not include any more prison breakouts. When I left Parchman, it would be by an official release and not an escape. As I went about my work in the chaplain's office, the weeks grew into months, and many of the doubters realized that I had, indeed, been changed.

In addition to my daily clerical duties in the chaplain's office, I accompanied the chaplains on their rounds to the various camps, helping with ministry and with Bible studies. I also periodically traveled with the chaplains, usually Chaplain Howell, on speaking engagements to churches around the state of Mississippi. Invitations came from churches of all sizes, mainly Baptist and Methodist. The chaplain would usually talk about the importance of ministering to those in prison, and I would talk about what God had done in my life. I enjoyed being able to bear witness to the life-changing power of Christ and explain the need for true faith and genuine repentance.

All seemed to be going well for me. Then, suddenly, Superintendent Collier resigned after less than a year on the job at Parchman. I heard that it was related to political conflicts with people in state government. It was a sad day to see him leave after such a hopeful beginning. He was succeeded by Mr. Bill Hollowell, a former sheriff and highway patrolman, who was quite security-conscious. The new superintendent took a dim view of my living behind his house with no security. Consequently, I was assigned to live and work at the pre-release center, where I would remain for the next four years.

The pre-release center was the next best place to live at Parchman prison. It was a minimum-security honor camp without fences or guards and only a couple of round-the-clock supervisory personnel. Parolees were sent there three weeks before release, to receive counseling and instruction during their transition from prison to free society.

Unlike an ordinary camp, pre-release was modeled more on the lines of a college dormitory. A deliberate effort was made to create as normal an environment as possible. The front door opened into a large, well-furnished and carpeted lounge area. This space opened into a modern cafeteria, forming the center of a building that had a wing on either side. The wing off of one side of the lounge contained a dormitory with modern bunk beds and bathrooms. The other wing housed a classroom and a suite of offices for the state's Division of Vocational Rehabilitation. Pre-release sat on a large grassy lot with no fences and had a lake about a hundred yards from the building. It wasn't a country club, but it was one of the nicest arrangements on the vast prison complex.

My new assignment consisted of assisting the vocational rehabilitation staff of four counselors and their secretaries. My initial duties were few and menial: making coffee twice a day, keeping the staff lounge clean, cleaning the bathrooms, making photocopies of documents, and so forth. Before long, I was asked to teach courses to the parolees, including a motivational course called "Success Through a Positive Mental Attitude." Another was "The World of Work," which centered on employer-employee relations. I also taught a driver's education course to help inmates get their driver's licenses before they left.

Not long thereafter, the chaplains' offices relocated to the pre-release center, and I once again served as their clerk under Chaplain Glenn Howell, in addition to my other duties. While there, I got to know the new chaplain for women, an older lady named Wendy Hatcher, a member of First Presbyterian Church in Cleveland, Mississippi. Because the female population was small and didn't require all of her time, she often spent time in the office doing administrative work. She turned out to be something of a spiritual mother to me. Seldom did a day pass without our discussing the Bible and the Christian life, and she was always bringing me religious books and tapes. She also brought various members of her prayer group (mainly women) to meet me, and they took an interest and began to pray for me regularly. Often it fell to her lot to pray and counsel me through times of doubt, confusion, and despair. (In spite of having had such a dramatic conversion experience, I went through a period of doubting my salvation.)

Much of this unsettledness came from my struggles with indwelling sin, especially pride, self-righteousness, a judgmental spirit, and various sinful thoughts and desires. I desired holiness, but I did not yet understand the intensity or dynamics of the lifelong battle with the world, the flesh, and the Devil. Nor did I understand how to consistently live the Christian life. It was easy to identify with Paul in Romans 7:22–24 when he said, "For I delight in the law of God, in my inner being, but I see in my members another law waging war against the law of my mind and making me captive to the law of sin that dwells in my members. Wretched man that I am! Who will deliver me from this body of death?" But I couldn't find my way to what he said a few verses later: "For the law of the Spirit of life has set you free in Christ Jesus from the law of sin and death" (8:2). Some days were good; others were bad. The cycle of ups and downs was unsettling and discouraging. And exposure to certain forms of "victorious life" teaching only made it worse.

Through her wise counsel and prayers, Wendy helped me get on a path of deepening growth in the Christian life by introducing me to spiritual classics—books such as *Studies in the Sermon on the Mount* by Martin Lloyd-Jones. Thankfully, she was patient with the perfectionism that I had developed from being the adult child of an alcoholic, something that would take quite a while to change.

Several months after I had moved to the pre-release center, the Reverend Ken Dean, who had visited me when I was in the maximum-security unit, returned to Mississippi from his seminary studies in New York. He had been involved in helping facilitate reconciliation between individuals and groups who were racially or politically alienated from one another, and he wanted to see if he could help me reconcile with some of my enemies, and they with me. To this end he suggested the possibility of my talking with Mr. Aaron Henry, the head of the Mississippi NAACP. Ken arranged a phone call for us, and it turned out to be a cordial conversation and a small step toward reconciliation with a leader in the black community, though we spoke only once. It wasn't much, but anytime people on opposite sides of an issue can speak cordially it is a small step that can draw them a bit closer and strengthen a foundation for further progress. A long series of small steps can eventually bridge large gaps if both sides are willing.

Ken also proposed a meeting with Mr. Alvin Binder. Al was a prominent criminal attorney in Jackson and a leader in Mississippi's Jewish community. When the Klan began its terror campaign against the Jews, he took a year off from his lucrative law practice to help the FBI stop it. A tough-minded, highly competent lawyer, he had played a crucial role in breaking up the Klan.

In a propitious coincidence, Frank Watts had worked closely with Binder on the Meridian bombings and knew him well. A few months before Ken Dean approached Al, Frank had also suggested a reconciliation meeting. Al's terse response was, "Let him rot in hell." With that rebuke in mind, I told Ken that if he thought he could persuade Binder and arrange it with prison officials, I would be glad to meet with him. But I was not optimistic. Nevertheless, a few weeks later Ken showed up at Parchman with my nemesis in tow. This was another momentous development that appeared insignificant at the time.

When Al and I first stood in front of each other, there was a suspicious and prickly tension between us. The air in the room was electric. He was a trial lawyer and fired questions at me to see if I would try to evade him or deceive him. I answered truthfully and directly. I told him how sorry I was for all I had done. I offered to make whatever amends I could. Once he realized I wasn't playing games, the tension gave way. When Al left that afternoon, we weren't good friends, but there was enough easing of the tension to call it a step toward reconciliation. Moreover, the foundation had been laid for what would eventually become a real friendship.

This moment marked my first rapprochement with a member of the Jewish community. I had made another effort before this. A couple of years earlier, Frank Watts had asked me if I would like him to arrange an opportunity for me to ask Meyer Davidson's forgiveness. I wanted to do it, but when Frank reached out to Davidson, he was not ready to consider it. I couldn't really blame him for feeling that way—it would be a difficult thing to give any credence to a so-called Christian who had tried to blow up his home then later claimed that he had been changed by Jesus and was actually a "real Christian" now. At least I could be grateful for the fact that in spite of all the terror I had inflicted on them, he and his family had not been physically harmed.

I continued to develop friendships across racial lines within the prison, however. Perhaps the most notable was Douglass Baker, a black civil rights lawyer who was serving a short term at Parchman. I first met Doug in 1973, I believe, when we served together on the prisoner advisory committee, a group established by prison officials to give input on how to improve conditions for inmates. An intelligent, cultured, and well-educated man, Doug was also a writer and an excellent classical pianist. He was passionate and outspoken in his racial and liberal political beliefs, but this did not hinder our friendship. For some reason, Doug genuinely liked me; I liked him too. Once again, a personal relationship shattered stereotypes I had once held so tightly. Shortly after Doug's release, he came to faith in Christ through a mutual friend of ours. We remained in periodic contact for a number of years after our prison days until he died.

I developed good friendships with two other interesting inmates. One was a college student who had been deeply involved in the drug scene. While in Parchman, he, too, came to know Christ. His life had changed dramatically. Another was a leftist who had formerly been a member of the far-left Students for a Democratic Society (SDS) and had gotten in trouble in Mississippi. He and I developed a friendly relationship, in spite of our earlier radical tendencies. He was a highly intelligent, quiet, mild-mannered guy, and I liked him a lot.

What an unexpected direction my life had taken! I had developed friendships with an FBI agent, a liberal civil rights leader, a Jewish leader, a militant civil rights lawyer, a hippie drug user, and a radical leftist. The alienation and hostility that once separated us was gone. This was a surprising and strange list of friends for a former Ku Klux Klan terrorist.

Not only is God in the business of reconciliation, but he has a sense of humor as well.

# NEW POSSIBILITIES

My time at the pre-release center was not without its dangers. One night a drunk inmate named Kenny got into a disagreement with another inmate and pulled a knife. The situation quickly escalated, and Kenny began chasing the other inmate through the center, intending to kill him. Fortunately, Kenny slowed down long enough for me to catch up and try to talk with him. To my surprise, he responded to me, and he gave me the knife. Minutes later, security officers arrived and took both men to maximum security. The subsequent investigation revealed that a corrupt guard had been smuggling in alcohol and selling it to the inmates. He was fired.

The incident may sound trivial in comparison to other events that had led me to this point, but it was not trivial at all. Those seemingly random circumstances had, in fact, saved my life. The leaders of the Mississippi Ku Klux Klan had heard of my conversion not just from me by letter but from newspaper accounts and others. To them, I had become a traitor to the Cause. And there's nothing extremists hate more than a traitor to their cause.

So the Klan had ordered a hit on me.

After several months in maximum security, Kenny returned to his job at the pre-release center. One of the first things he did was thank me for keeping him from killing the other inmate. In gratitude, he then made a bone-chilling confession. His attorney was a man whom I knew, and who had been deeply involved with the Klan. Kenny said that days before the knife incident, this lawyer had sent an intermediary to the pre-release center on visiting day to offer him $2,500 (which was a lot of money to a prisoner in those days) to ensure that I had a "fatal accident."

The night I stopped him from killing the other inmate, he actually had the opportunity to kill me. But when he realized I had intervened for his benefit, out of concern for him—an angry, drunk convict with a grievance and a knife—he decided not to hurt me.

It was another instance of God intervening to protect my life.

*     *     *

By the summer of 1974, I had read almost every book that I could obtain on my must-read list. I had also taken what college courses I could by correspondence, although in the mid-seventies there weren't many available that interested me. To continue my education would require both the structure and the resources of a university.

That, in turn, would require me to be out of prison.

I think Frank Watts first raised the prospect of my early release. He based this on the profound changes in my beliefs, life, and attitudes, and my demonstrated commitment to follow Jesus. In conversations with his superiors at the FBI, Frank argued that I was no longer a radical, no longer a risk, and that I was far more valuable to society on the outside, where I could share how God had changed me from a hate-filled racist to a follower of Christ. Maybe I could be useful in turning young people away from being radicalized, he reasoned.

However, Frank's supervisors at the FBI flatly disagreed. They still saw me as a dangerous criminal. Word came down (I'm not sure if it was from Hoover or from Roy Moore, the special agent in charge for Mississippi) that if Frank liked his job and wanted to keep it, he ought to give up this idea. As far as the FBI was concerned, I was where I was supposed to be.

I had told Ken Dean of my desire to attend college, and he encouraged it, saying he'd talk to Bill Hollowell, the superintendent. Hollowell responded positively and said that at the proper time he would present the matter to the new governor, Bill Waller, who would have to give final approval. Hollowell also pointed out that I had no chance at early release unless leaders of Mississippi's black community and Jewish community agreed to support it, or at least not oppose it. Then Ken called Lieutenant Governor William Winter, who was a personal friend of his. Ken also spoke with key white liberals and leaders of the black community to assure them of my changed life.

The prison's staff psychologist gave me a thorough psychological evaluation and concluded that my rehabilitation was complete. He even drove me to Jackson to take the Scholastic Aptitude Test (SAT). Along with the prison's assistant superintendent, he wrote letters of recommendation to the colleges where I applied. Through his encouragement and that of Ken Dean and Henry Barmettler, I applied to and was accepted at Rutgers College in New Jersey, Duke University in North Carolina, and Earlham College in Indiana. Everything was falling into place. I had made high SAT scores, been accepted by three excellent schools, and been recommended by Parchman's psychologist and executive staff. My former enemies had agreed to my release, and even the lieutenant governor was ready to publicly support it.

But when the proposal came to Governor Waller, his answer was a firm no. In a televised news conference, someone asked him about the possibility of my early release, and the governor said that while I had made considerable progress during my years in Parchman, he felt it was not yet time for me to be released from incarceration.

I was devastated. Why hadn't God intervened and opened the door for my release? Why had he not blessed my efforts and those of my friends? Why had he not answered my prayers and those of many others on my behalf? What we were seeking and praying for was good, not bad. Wasn't six years in prison enough? There seemed no hope left for an early release. To me, if this effort failed, as strong as it was, no effort would succeed. The future looked very dark, even hopeless. I would be stuck at Parchman for many more years.

To make matters worse, I was teaching classes full of inmates who were about to be released, most of whom had no intention of going straight. I didn't dispute that I deserved my sentence. But I was a new man, and I would never be involved in crime again, while two-thirds of these men would be back in prison in three years or less. It was hard. Very hard. My hopes were crushed. The future looked bleak.

For several days I had to fight strong feelings of bitterness, resentment, self-pity, and depression. But gradually I realized that, among other things, this disappointment was to show me a simple but important truth: "For my thoughts are not your thoughts, neither are your ways my ways, declares the LORD. For as the heavens are higher than the earth, so are my ways higher than your ways and my thoughts than your thoughts" (Isaiah 55:8–9).

As I prayed through this crisis of faith, God impressed on me in a clear, unmistakable way that he would eventually set me free, but that it would be in his time and on his terms. I was to make no further efforts to bring it about in my own strength. One day he spoke to me as clearly as I have ever experienced in my life. It was just as clear, strong, and distinct as if someone were speaking to me audibly, but without any sound. He said to me, "Stop trying to get out. You can't get out a day sooner than I want you to leave, and they can't hold you a day longer than I want you to stay." This was not what I wanted to hear, but it was what I needed to hear. It stabilized me. My hope returned. I had to trust God and wait patiently for him to act in his own time.

Two years later, in the spring of 1976, I met Dr. Leighton Ford, an evangelist with the Billy Graham Evangelistic Association. Dr. Ford came to the area as part of an evangelistic crusade, and when he came to the prison to preach, we had a brief talk—the beginning of what grew to be a good friendship.

After our conversation, Ford concluded that it would be good for me to attend Chuck Colson's prison discipleship program in Washington, DC. The two-week program was designed to provide intensive discipleship training for inmates who wanted to grow spiritually and were trusted by prison chaplains. First Presbyterian church generously offered to cover any expense involved. Ford contacted Chuck Colson, who sent a letter to prison officials asking that I be allowed to participate in the Washington program.

This was a highly unusual request, especially for someone as politically controversial as I was. (Skeptics were still around.) The warden and staff were supportive, but a request of this nature—leaving the state for two weeks unescorted—had to be approved by the governor himself. Then there was the additional issue that the program had no security; everything was based on the honor system. Complicating matters further was the fact that Mississippi had a newly elected governor. It was a long shot, but the Parchman officials forwarded Chuck Colson's invitation, with the warden's personal recommendation for approval, to Governor Cliff Finch.

Given that I had a thirty-year sentence for terrorism, plus five years more for escaping, Governor Finch would certainly see me as a security risk. Even if I didn't escape, once it became known that he had approved my leaving the state for two weeks without supervision, there could well be a public uproar. And if I did escape, there was no way he could defend his decision. Getting permission was extremely unlikely. But the prison chaplains and I prayed that if it was God's will for me to go to Washington, he would open the door. We waited and waited, but no word came.

Through a set of circumstances that can only be described as miraculous, Governor Cliff Finch gave his approval. On the last possible day, a state senator who was a good friend of the governor's top aide, Herman Glazier, was visiting the prison and came to the pre-release center for a tour. Chaplain Howell was showing him around and introduced me to him, taking the opportunity to explain my problem. The man called Mr. Glazier in the governor's office on the spot and the approval was forthcoming. I was going to Washington, DC.

During my two weeks at Chuck Colson's Prison Fellowship Discipleship Program, I got to know a dozen other inmates—all from federal prisons. The program provided teaching during the day and visits to churches on Sundays and several weekday evenings. For me, it was a time of solid teaching and spiritual growth. It was also the beginning of long-lasting and rewarding friendships with four special men who taught in the program: Chuck Colson, Sen. Harold Hughes, Dr. Richard Halverson, and Dr. John Staggers.

Chuck Colson was a conservative Republican, former marine captain, high-powered Washington lawyer, special counsel to President Richard Nixon, and White House hatchet man who had spent seven months in prison for his involvement in the Watergate conspiracy. He, too, had experienced a remarkable transformation, one that produced a passion to help those in prison.

Harold Hughes was a liberal Democrat who had been the governor of Iowa and United States senator from 1969 to 1975 and loved Jesus Christ. He had a strong commitment to helping the poor and people struggling with alcoholism, with which he once suffered. He was a bear of a man who had traveled a hard path through life. He understood the common man and his problems and tried to do what he could to help people. He was not a typical Washington politician and left the Senate after only one term in order to serve God in other ways.

Dr. Halverson, senior pastor of Fourth Presbyterian Church and chairman of the board of World Vision, was a highly respected evangelical leader in the United States and abroad.

Dr. John Staggers, a former assistant to the mayor of Washington and former professor at Howard University, was a respected black leader. He played a courageous role in calming the riots in Washington after the assassination of Dr. Martin Luther King Jr., walking into a group of angry, armed rioters to reduce tensions and challenge them to work for change through nonviolent means. One of the most remarkable things about these four men was the fact that in spite of their differences, they were good friends because of their relationship with Christ. They had a unity in Christ and worked together to serve him.

In a group discernment exercise toward the end of this two-week program, each inmate was asked to share what spiritual gifts we saw in the others. I was identified by several as having a gift of teaching. From then on, I began to wonder about ministry. Might God want to use me in a ministry of teaching and helping others grow as disciples of Jesus?

The high point of the conference came the night before we returned to our respective prisons. A banquet was held at a grand old mansion in the Embassy Row section of Washington, DC, as a commencement service for the men in the discipleship program.

Before dinner, Chuck Colson came into the kitchen, where I was talking with someone, and told me he wanted to introduce me to a man who was in the library. It was Eldridge Cleaver, a man who had been a leader in the Black Panther Party, an organization committed to armed struggle against racism and the United States government. FBI director J. Edgar Hoover had described the Black Panthers as "the greatest threat to internal security of the country."[1] In 1968, Cleaver had fled prosecution in Oakland, California, for the attempted murder of two policemen, going first to Cuba, then Algeria, and eventually France. He had recently returned to the United States after renouncing his radical past and professing faith in Christ.

I had heard of Eldridge's rather unusual conversion experience, which I couldn't quite understand, and wanted to meet him. As Chuck and I left the kitchen together, I jokingly asked him, "Are you sure this guy's saved?" Quite amused, he assured me there was nothing to worry about, and we went downstairs to the library. A more dissimilar group than you could possibly imagine now stood together in that library—Chuck Colson, Harold Hughes, Eldridge Cleaver, and Tom Tarrants. A moment later I found myself shaking hands with a man I would have hated several years before, but for whom I now felt only love. Under any other circumstances, those of us around the table would have been at least ideological enemies. But because of a common commitment to Jesus Christ, it could now be different for all of us. Sadly, Eldridge got on the speaker circuit before becoming well-grounded in the faith and wound up becoming disillusioned and spiraling into a bizarre course of life.

I did not realize at the time the significance of what God was doing. He was continuing to work out his great plan of reconciliation— reconciliation of man to God and man to man—through the power of Christ. He was also strengthening my spiritual life and laying the foundation of my future ministry.

# FREE AT LAST!

N ot long after my return from Washington, a federal court order to
reduce overcrowding at Parchman made it possible for me to be
considered for a work-release program. The inmate population at that
point was 2,600 and rising, well above the designated maximum capacity
of 1,900. The court gave the state of Mississippi a limited window of time
to comply with the reduction order. This greatly favored my situation. If
approved, I could possibly be released by Christmas of that year.

Without my prompting, two counselors in the Division of Vocational
Rehabilitation took it on themselves to do the early groundwork. In
preparation for work release, I had to pass a thorough psychological
evaluation and pass muster, in person, before the prison classification
committee. Then there was the matter of securing a job and sponsor in
Mississippi. Often, an inmate's family would help arrange this, but since
mine was 350 miles away in Alabama and had no contacts in Mississippi,
they couldn't help.

Under the terms of the work-release program, the county sheriff and chief circuit judge in whatever jurisdiction I chose to relocate would have to give their official approval. A number of people in nearby Cleveland, only twenty-five miles away, had befriended me and it also had a good university, so I decided to apply there. Most of my friends were leaders in the community, and I assumed their recommendations would assure approval. But during my two years of waiting, I had learned to look first to God and seek his will. So I prayed that if this wasn't where God wanted me to go, he would shut the door. And the door closed before my eyes. The sheriff refused to approve my coming to Cleveland. I was disappointed, but this time I was not crushed.

I applied to go to Tupelo, Mississippi, hometown of Elvis Presley, where I also had some Christian friends. Again, I prayed that God would close this door if it were not his place for me. And again, local officials refused to accept me.

My relocation from Parchman was going to be more difficult than I thought. I was at one time labeled by the press and federal and state authorities as the most dangerous man in Mississippi. That stuck in people's minds. More important, my crime had involved shooting a police officer—an extremely serious offense in its own right. Even though I was no longer the terrorist who had been the FBI's number one target in Mississippi, not everyone knew that. It would be politically risky for a sheriff and judge to approve my living in their jurisdiction. Even if local citizens did not protest, law enforcement authorities would. For some people I was barely human and should rot in prison.

On the day I learned of my rejection by authorities in Tupelo, I was scheduled to speak to a class of law enforcement students visiting from the University of Mississippi. Tour groups regularly visited the pre-release center to see the facilities, eat lunch in the cafeteria, and talk with the inmates. The prison tour guide, Mrs. McBride, had arranged for me to address the group and answer their questions. At the end of my talk, she mentioned to the group that because of political issues I was having trouble finding a county to accept me on work release. It turned out that the professor leading the class on the tour, Dr. Chester Quarles, happened to be director of the University of Mississippi's law enforcement program. After hearing my story, he took an interest in my situation and later offered to recommend me to the circuit judge, district attorney, sheriff, and chief of police in Oxford, where Ole Miss was located. What's more, he said he would try to find me a part-time job. I later discovered that he was active in his church and missions work.

This time, step-by-step, everything fell into place, as if an unseen hand was guiding the process, and my application for admission to the University of Mississippi was accepted. Thanks to the sustained efforts of the two counselors in the Division of Vocational Rehabilitation office, I received both state and federal grants to help cover expenses. Oxford officials gave their approval, and I was offered a part-time job.

This door was definitely looking open.

By Monday, December 6, 1976, everything had been completed except the Oxford parole officer's report, which had to verify my job, sponsor, and living arrangements. Once this was in, Parchman's brand-new superintendent, John Watkins, and the state commissioner of corrections, Dr. Allen Ault, would review my case.

Disapproval at any level would block my release.

Although I was hopeful, I knew it would not be a slam dunk. Several months earlier, a number of my friends and mentors had written the governor, asking for my sentence to be reduced to make me eligible for release. The governor's office forwarded the request to the parole board. After weighing the matter at length, the parole board recommended that no clemency be granted at that time. (I was told that my case was a political "hot potato," and they did not want to touch it.) Their no-clemency report arrived in the governor's office just days before I was to be considered for the work-release program. My prospects for release seemed dim.

The federal court's deadline for reducing the prison population was December 31, 1976. On December 8, Dr. Ault, who was new on the job, was scheduled to be at the prison to oversee the review of inmate records. But my papers were still incomplete. The parole officer at Oxford had not yet made his routine investigation, much less written his report. It looked as though I would run out of time before my case could be considered.

That morning, Ed McBride, a top administrator at Parchman telephoned the parole officer in Oxford and asked if he could complete the investigation before noon. Ed, who was a pilot, then flew his personal plane the ninety miles to Oxford, met the parole officer at the airport to get the necessary papers, and flew back to Parchman in time to put my now-completed package in front of the review committee. Dr. Ault and Superintendent Watkins agreed to interview me that afternoon.

At about 1:00 p.m., I was told to get ready to go to the warden's office. This was going to be the big day for me. I immediately asked Chaplain Wendy Hatcher to ask some of my closest friends to be in prayer.

In the midst of the excitement and tension, I felt a deep peace. I was able to pray with an honest heart that God's perfect will would prevail. I wanted very much to be free, but more than that, I wanted whatever God wanted—even if it meant spending more time in prison. It was hard to pray, "Not my will, but yours, be done." But I was somehow enabled to do it.

The guards came and drove me from pre-release to the administration building, a distance of several miles. What a strange feeling it was as I looked out across the brown fields to realize that the long-awaited day might have finally come. We pulled in front of the building and entered the warden's outer office. In a few moments a tall, neatly dressed man in his late forties came out and introduced himself as Superintendent John Watkins. He invited me into his office, where he introduced me to Dr. Allen Ault. Mr. Watkins was a well-educated, confident man with a forceful personality. He began asking me questions while Dr. Ault sat quietly to one side, almost out of my sight. The questions came fast and varied. Sometimes I could follow his line of thinking; other times it seemed to come out of the blue.

He opened with "What was it like growing up?" and moved on to "How did you get yourself in so much trouble with the law?" Then, with no show of emotion, "And why did you break out of prison? Hadn't you learned anything from the trouble you got into?"

The rapid-fire questions probably lasted for about half an hour, but it seemed longer than that. I felt as if I were being interrogated by a skilled intelligence officer. At times he would question me as a psychologist, at times as a sociologist, yet always as a skeptic.

Suddenly the questioning stopped and there was silence in the room. I could read body language well enough to see that Superintendent Watkins had made his decision. I held my breath.

"I'm an atheist," he declared. "I've been in this work too long to have any confidence at all in your 'religion.' In all my years in corrections, I have known only one man who got religion in prison and kept it after he left. I wouldn't release you on the strength of your religion, because I don't think it's worth five cents. And I think you will discard it when you get out. But I do believe you have changed and deserve a chance to make something of yourself. That's why I'm going to release you."

I felt a flood of emotions welling up in me. My waiting was over. There would be no more suspense. Somehow, I held on to the peace I had when I walked into his office.

Dr. Ault then spoke. "Will Monday next week be soon enough to leave?"

I turned to Dr. Ault and said, "Yes, sir. Monday will be just fine."

As I left the warden's office, friends on the staff who had been sweating out my interview came up to learn the decision. When I told them the news, they were overjoyed. But the person who was the most overjoyed and most thankful was not there that day. My dear mother, who had put her hope and trust in God and prayed faithfully for all those years, was filled with joy when I called to tell her the news.

What none of us knew at the time was that the political sensitivities of my case meant that the governor had to give final approval to the decision that had just been made. As he pondered the decision, he sought advice from his special counsel, a friend of many years whose judgment he could trust. The special counsel said, "I know this man and believe that he is a real Christian now. I recommend that you release him." The special counsel was Alvin Binder, the Jewish lawyer I had earlier come to know through Ken Dean.

Chaplain Glenn Howell drove me back to the pre-release center. He had come to Parchman only weeks after I had found Christ. He and his family had prayed for, encouraged, and supported me all these years, through the ups and downs of prison life. Truly, God had brought him to Parchman, at least in part, to walk with me during that time. How grateful I was—and still am—for his friendship and wisdom.

On my last night in prison—Sunday, December 12, 1976—Glenn and his wife, Mary, gave a going-away party for me at their home. There on the prison grounds, friends from around Mississippi came to see me for the last time at Parchman. It was an emotional time for all of us—a time of joy and gratitude in remembering God's past blessings as well as anticipating those to come.

Tokens of future blessings were already appearing. When I had walked into the warden's office on Wednesday, I had fifty dollars to my name. By Sunday, various friends had chipped in more than a thousand dollars (which was a lot of money in those days). Frank and Joyce Watts had arranged to provide me a new wardrobe. And of course, my mother wanted to provide anything else I needed. I would leave prison with everything I needed to start a new chapter of my life.

The next morning, December 13, 1976, dawned bright and crisp and clear. At about 8:30 a.m., a prison station wagon arrived at the pre-release center where I had spent the last four years. I said good-bye to my fellow inmates, who had to remain behind and wait for their turn. As I turned to leave the center for the last time, I realized I had been in Parchman prison exactly eight years to the day from the time I had arrived.

When we arrived at the identification office for out-processing, I found that it had been moved into a new, modern facility that very morning. Nonetheless, the sergeant in charge was the same man who'd admitted me to Parchman eight years before. He seemed genuinely glad to see me getting out. He shook my hand and wished me well.

Dr. Quarles and his wife had come to Parchman to drive me to Oxford and the University of Mississippi. Colorful Christmas decorations filled the windows of the houses along guard row just as they had been that December evening eight years earlier. I was struck by the contrast. That was a day of deepening gloom and bleak despair. This was a new day of hope and freedom. I could feel the joy of Christmas. Yet the greatest contrast that morning was not in my circumstances, but in me. I was not the same man.

# Part 2
# SEEING GOD WORK IN THE ORDINARY

1977–2019

# 18 OLE MISS: A HAPPY CHANGE

When I left prison in 1976, racial conflict in America had decreased compared to the previous decade. In Mississippi and elsewhere, the Klan was nothing like it once was. And the civil rights legislation of the 1960s had given hope to many people that the plight of blacks would improve along with race relations in general. White resistance to civil rights gains was diminishing steadily. Like many, I assumed the worst was behind us and things would continue to get better over time. My focus was now on getting an education in preparation for ministry of some sort. It never occurred to me that part of that ministry might be in the area of racial reconciliation. Nor was I aware that in prison God had put me into a long-term training program in how to understand and love people who were very different from me. The journey that was unfolding before me would be one with unexpected twists and turns but with profoundly positive effects on my life.

As Dr. and Mrs. Quarles and I drove toward Ole Miss, the brown cotton fields of the flat Mississippi delta gave way to the evergreen rolling hills of north central Mississippi. My new life was unfolding before my eyes. It was still only barely believable that I would be able to study at the University of Mississippi and move forward with my goal of serving God. My heart was overflowing with hope and excitement. My future, once bleak, was now growing brighter with every mile of distance between me and Parchman.

Leaving prison is fraught with danger for most former inmates. A prisoner may be set free, but with that freedom comes the responsibility of making new choices. We make our choices; then our choices make us. For most prisoners, successful reintegration into society is not easy. The rate of recidivism is high. Two-thirds of released prisoners are rearrested within three years. I was determined not to be one of them.

Before my arrest and conviction, I had made some terrible choices. The question—my challenge—was whether I would now make the right choices and adjust to normal society after eight years in prison.

I believed that if I tried to live a life that pleased God, he would help me through whatever challenges were ahead. I was still a work in progress, and that gave me pause. But I also knew the Lord was merciful and gracious and was working in my life. While I was in prison, he had blessed me with a great support system in the form of people who believed in me and helped me. Now that I was free, he would do the same. With the support of a good church and mature believers, the process of transformation could accelerate.

I also had my family. It was not perfect by any means. While I was in prison, my parents had divorced, and I was alienated from my father. But in spite of this, they were honest, hardworking people who loved me and my siblings, took good care of us, sent us to church, demonstrated good values, and taught us the difference between right and wrong. In short, they did the best they could. Thus, despite the wrong turns that defined my youth, I had a foundation of decent values to which I could return and build. And I had a praying mother. Augustine said of his mother, "I cannot sufficiently express the love she had for me, nor how she now travailed for me in the spirit with a far keener anguish than when she bore me in the flesh."[1] The same was true for me!

In this, I was very fortunate. Most inmates have no such foundation.

*     *     *

Oxford, Mississippi, was a small, charming, and picturesque town with the county courthouse at the center of a town square. The square was surrounded by several blocks of small businesses, shops, and restaurants. Beyond them were homes and then the campus, only a few blocks away. The people of Oxford were friendly and welcoming. For its size, it had more than its share of educated, cultured people who were interested in music, the arts, and so on.

The campus itself was graceful and serene, full of students walking here and there in pursuit of their studies. At the heart of the campus, on University Circle, stood the Lyceum, a large and stately Greek Revival structure. The Lyceum overlooked a grassy, tree-shaded area of several acres known as the Grove, where students met, talked, and hung out.

No one would ever have guessed that fourteen years earlier students on this same campus had reacted with deadly violence to the admission of James Meredith, the first black person to attend Ole Miss. As I scanned the campus in December 1976, there was no evidence, at least not overt evidence, of that racism. As far as I could see, whites and blacks attended classes together without problems. In my former life, I would have seen this as compromise, but now I saw it as a sign of progress and was glad. Ole Miss was precisely the right university for me.

I spent the Christmas holidays as a house guest of Dr. Quarles and his family and enjoyed getting to know them. Dr. Quarles would watch over and counsel me for the rest of my time at the university.

Once school resumed for the spring semester, I moved into campus housing. Dormitory living was a good experience. I had three great roommates. We got along well, which was a blessing. We had rich fellowship during our time together. One eventually became a lawyer, another became a businessman, and the third went to seminary and became a pastor.

My part-time job was also a blessing. I worked a few hours each week at a movie theater within walking distance of the campus. I couldn't have asked for a better situation. A few months later, my mother bought me a car, which opened up new work possibilities. Now that I was mobile, Dr. Quarles offered me a better-paying job at a private security company that he owned. I worked as an unarmed security guard at a nearby manufacturing plant. I checked worker ID badges during the afternoon shift and directed any visitors to appropriate offices. This took relatively little time and left me several hours on each shift to do homework.

Adjusting to life as a free man was proving to be less difficult than I had expected. It was exhilarating just to be alive and free. Prison life had been drab, dull, and gray, with numbing routines. Now, as I walked around campus, I was overcome by the beauty of God's creation—green grass, the flowers, the great oak trees, and the blue sky. I felt alive in a way I had not felt in a very long time. I had been in prison from age twenty-one to twenty-nine, and I had been in intellectual bondage for several years before that. Having been given a second chance was yet another in a series of miracles that had brought me to this point.

One of my main concerns initially was where to attend church. After visiting several, I settled on College Hill Presbyterian Church. I met students and leaders there from campus ministries such as Navigators, InterVarsity, and Campus Crusade for Christ. Becoming part of such a community of faith was a stabilizing force in my life.

I found that I loved academics. Ole Miss provided me with the structure and the intellectual resources I had needed. I had come to Ole Miss to study, and I thrived there. I had no interest in the partying or football games for which the school was famous. My chief goal was to prepare to serve God in some way, and I remained focused on that. While in prison, I had taken a couple of correspondence courses from the Moody Bible Institute in New Testament Greek, which enabled me to test out of first-year Greek and start with second year. I decided to major in Classics, with its focus on Greco-Roman culture and languages. I was especially eager to improve my ability to read the New Testament in Greek and to understand it better.

I devoted myself to my studies and to my involvement in church and campus ministries. My understanding and choices were being formed by what I read in the Bible and through the influence of men and women further along in the faith than me. I had much to learn about God's grace, far more than I realized at the time. But at least I was on the way.

One day, I got a phone call from Leighton Ford, who earlier had encouraged Chuck Colson to invite me to attend his prison discipleship program in Washington, DC. Leighton invited me to speak at an evangelistic crusade he was soon to lead in the Chicago area. I did so, and afterward Leighton asked me to join him for dinner with Billy Graham, his brother-in-law, who was in town at that time. What a privilege it was to speak at an evangelistic crusade and then have dinner with Billy Graham, who, in spite of all his fame, remained a very humble man.

Not long after that, Leighton called again. Billy was wondering if I might be open to having my story turned into a movie through his World Wide Pictures production company. This caught me by surprise, and I asked for time to pray about it. As I did, God impressed his answer on my mind very clearly. The answer was "No. If you try to build yourself up, I will tear you back down." This seemed strange to me, since a movie could reach many more people than I ever could by just speaking to groups. Logically, it didn't make sense. Plus, I didn't think I had a problem with pride (though, like most people who struggle with pride, I did but was unaware of it). I continued praying and got the same answer: no. I called Leighton and declined.

The Lord also had much more to teach me about race, and it started at Ole Miss. One of the students I met through a campus ministry event was S. T., a quiet, somewhat reserved African American. He and I became good friends and found each other's company mutually encouraging. Another friend was Eddie, an engineering student from Africa. But the most unusual friendship of all was the one that developed with Nadim, an engineering student from the Middle East who spent most of his time with a couple of other engineering students from the Middle East. Nadim and I enjoyed each other, and he soon introduced me to his friends, who wanted to know more about America and Americans. I found them to be nice guys who were serious about their studies, and I invited them to attend church with me, which they did.

I learned a bit more about Jewish people, too, through Al Binder. Our relationship continued after I left prison, mainly through occasional phone calls. An interesting and humorous exception was a chance encounter at the Governor's Prayer Breakfast in Jackson, Mississippi. I had been invited and was in a small gathering the night before with Dr. Tom Skinner, an African American leader whose friendship and wisdom would later have a significant impact on me. For some reason, Al happened into the meeting. When he saw me, he got excited and starting telling everybody how I had become a real Christian. It was amazing, gratifying, and humorous all at the same time!

During this period, I also got to know Frank and Joyce Watts better, making several trips to the Mississippi Gulf Coast to visit them in Gulfport, where they now lived. Frank had been one of the first law enforcement officers to question me in jail after my arrest in Meridian. Our friendship, which started after he was born again, had grown deeper as time went on. My visits gave opportunities to get acquainted with his sons, meet some of their church friends, and speak to their congregation.

Good food, rich conversations, and attempted waterskiing were also part of our times together.

On my first trip to visit Frank and Joyce, I also met with my dad, who had moved to Gulfport a couple of years earlier. We went out to dinner, and I told him how sorry I was for my hateful, rebellious ways and all the trouble I had caused him and the family. I asked him to forgive me, and he did without hesitation and never mentioned it again. This marked a turning point in our relationship, and things improved between us in the years that followed.

Surprisingly, he and my mother later remarried, and he turned out to be a very good grandfather. A few years before he died in 1998, he came to faith in Jesus through the ministry of a faithful Baptist pastor, who took the time to make a home visit and share the gospel with him. This was a wonderful answer to decades of prayer by his mother and his wife and children. On his deathbed, his last request of me was to take care of my mother after he died, which I assured him I would do.

After I had been at Ole Miss for a while, a friend at church, who was a gifted writer, persuaded me that my story could glorify God and help many people. I agreed, believing that it could help people see the dangers of nominal Christianity, how political ideology distorts biblical faith, and the fallacies of racism and anti-Semitism. We collaborated on a book titled *The Conversion of a Klansman*. We knew that this could be dangerous if it aroused the anger of the Klan, but we decided to trust God and do it anyway.

I loved Ole Miss. I was thriving in its halls and classrooms. The academic environment suited me. But once my book manuscript was turned over to the publisher, I began to think more about possible consequences of its publication. The book wasn't exactly the kind of publicity the Ku Klux Klan appreciated. It was sure to enrage them. The more I thought about it, the more certain I was that they would likely attempt reprisals against me. The Klan had already tried to have me murdered in prison, and I was a far more accessible target at Ole Miss. Perhaps I would be better off moving elsewhere, to a place like Washington, DC, where I had some friends.

While I was pondering this, an acquaintance gave me some of the most important advice of my life, saying I had to choose between two options: I could get on the evangelical speaker circuit and probably become a sensation, or I could keep a low profile and focus on learning the Bible, growing as a disciple of Jesus, and helping others grow as his disciples. The first option would be dazzling for a short time but ultimately would produce little of lasting spiritual value. The second would keep me relatively unknown but over time would produce much fruit in people's lives.

I had a strong desire to help others grow into disciples of Jesus who would know, trust, love, and obey him. I also knew that getting on the speaker circuit and becoming a celebrity would only feed pride, compromising my own discipleship. My passion was to be useful, not conspicuous; the right decision was obvious.

I didn't like the idea of leaving Ole Miss without having completed my degree, but it was clear that I should trust God for what he had in store for me in Washington, DC. This was a big step of faith for me. As an ex-convict and former terrorist from Mississippi, thirty-one years old, and without a college degree, how would I fit into the nation's capital, a city filled with smart, powerful, important people? In many ways it did not make sense, yet a few days before I was to leave, God gave me a confirmation that I was making the right decision. Frank and Joyce Watts called me to say that God had told them to give me a car. It was a late-model Audi that one of their sons decided he didn't want, and it would be a great replacement for my tiny old Volkswagen Beetle. This completely unexpected and totally undeserved gift was a great encouragement to my faith as I ventured into the unknown world of the nation's capital.

# A NEW DIRECTION

I left the University of Mississippi for Washington, DC, with the intention of working in a ministry of discipleship while completing my undergraduate degree in classics at the George Washington University. Beyond that I had few details. But I was confident that God was leading me and would take care of me and work out his plans for my life.

Little did I know that his plans included exposure to a wide range of peoples and places that would expand my perspective on life and change me in significant ways. Mark Twain once said, "Travel is fatal to prejudice, bigotry, and narrow-mindedness, and many of our people need it sorely on these accounts. Broad, wholesome, charitable views of men and things cannot be acquired by vegetating in one little corner of the earth all of one's life."[1] That was certainly true for me.

I now believe this is one of the reasons why God led me to relocate to Washington, DC, with its very diverse population. I would meet people from a wide variety of backgrounds. Some of them would become friends, and those friendships would grow deeper and enrich me personally. My understanding of people, life, and the world would grow and many stereotypes would be shattered. Through the friendships that would develop, I would gain deeper understanding and insight into what life is like for people who are very different from me.

This began soon after I arrived, when I reestablished contact with Dr. John Staggers, whom I had met when in Washington for Chuck Colson's prison discipleship program. John was working at the all-black Third Street Church of God, just a few blocks from the Capitol. Among other things, he was helping lead Urban Breakfast, a ministry for the homeless that brought together the well-off and the down-and-out. John was a heavy, jovial man and welcomed me with a warm (and loud) "Hey mate!" and gave me a big bear hug. He took an interest in me and gave me good advice in my early days in DC. I remember him cautioning me one day that Washington is filled with people who have agendas and that I needed to be alert to people who might want to use me for their own ends. It was good advice. Our relationship would deepen in the years ahead and he would introduce me to others over time.

My first experience in full-time ministry was at a local university in the suburbs. Teaching and discipling students filled my days, and I loved it. It was an exciting, energizing, and fruitful period of ministry. But in time I came to see my need for more training, so I began to look into the possibility of attending seminary. Even though I had yet not completed my undergraduate degree, I was admitted to seminary as a special student. After demonstrating academic competency for a couple of semesters, I was allowed to transition into the master of divinity track, an option for people over thirty years of age.

During my time in seminary, I learned a lot more about the nature of true discipleship; the church; the importance of community, humility, and servanthood; and much more. And just as important, I saw it lived in daily life. I also learned about the importance of cultural analysis and of

discovering the unacknowledged assumptions that influence our thinking and behavior and the church. My eyes were opened as never before,
and my sense of mission grew. After all that Christ had done for me, what
would I do for him?

After seminary, God renewed my call to the Washington area to
"seek the welfare of the city" (Jeremiah 29:7), though in what capacity I did not yet know. Dr. Richard Halverson, who I had first met at
Chuck Colson's prisoners' discipleship program, advised me to start at
the bottom and let God take me wherever he wanted me to go. So at his
suggestion, I began attending a weekly prayer meeting held in the base-
ment of the Martin Luther King Jr. Memorial Library and led by John
Staggers and Congressman Tony Hall. The meeting drew an eclectic
assortment of about twenty to forty people from around Washington:
men and women, black and white, pastors, ministry leaders, business-
people, congressional staff, government workers, prayer warriors, a few
homeless people, and occasional visitors from other cities. This further
expanded my horizons and kept me from vegetating "in one little corner
of the earth."[2]

I attended almost every week for about five years, praying for the
needs of the city's people, including food for the hungry, housing for the
homeless, deliverance from drugs and violence, racial harmony, issues in
government, and revival in the churches. I got to know people who were
directly involved in trying to address these problems. Being part of this
group opened my eyes even more to the needs of the city's poor and needy.
And one of the pastors I met there would later play a significant role in
my life by inviting me to co-pastor with him in a city church.

Before I took that step, however, some friends and I helped start and
lead the School for Urban Missions. This was an accredited, semester-
long, off-campus study program for college students who were interested
in missions in the urban world. The inner city of Washington, DC, was
our base, learning laboratory, and place of service. The curriculum was

focused on missions, discipleship, spiritual formation, and hands-on learning. Students loved it.

While on a recruiting trip to Geneva College in Pennsylvania, I met Dr. John Perkins, who invited me to speak to a group of black students that he was due to address that afternoon. As I shared my story with the group, we transitioned to an open, honest conversation on race and grace that led to a warm friendship with John.

John had been active in the civil rights struggle in Mississippi, fighting for what I had been fighting against. His brother had been murdered by a white policeman. When he tried to investigate, white officers had beaten him nearly to death. All of this had provoked him to anger and hatred. But by God's grace, John survived and had been enabled to forgive his enemies and come to a place of loving white people.

John and I eventually coauthored a book telling our stories in alternating chapters and concluding with a section on racial reconciliation. The book grew out of a mutual desire to address the widespread prejudice in the church. John and I hoped to show that the gospel of Christ could indeed overcome the barriers of race, economics, and class that divide us. And through John's work and that of a number of business, political, and church leaders in Mississippi who share this vision, change has been quietly progressing in the state—notably so among churches composed of millennials.

After a year and a half of directing the School for Urban Missions, I was called to serve as co-pastor of a church in Washington, DC.[3] Predominantly white but with a mix of black and Hispanic believers as well, the congregation reflected the culture of the city, with people from the worlds of government and business mingling with the poor and even a few homeless folks. This experience continued to stretch me and move me out of my comfort zone. Preaching, teaching, and helping people with their problems was a joy, helping offset the stress and pressure I lived with in such a role.

Opportunities to be involved in encouraging racial reconciliation in DC continued to arise. I was able to bring together a group of Washington pastors to hear John Perkins speak on the topic. I was also able to bring John's son Spencer and his friend Chris Rice to speak at the church about their work on reconciliation across racial lines in their own church in Mississippi. Their book, *More than Equals: Racial Healing for the Sake of the Gospel*, had made a powerful impact on me, and I was eager for others to learn from them.

Then one day, in the midst of busy pastoral ministry, I received a phone call from an acquaintance in Mississippi, who forwarded an email from Officer Tom Tucker, the driver of the police cruiser that chased me down in Meridian. Our first meeting had been in the middle of a furious hail of gunfire.

His email began, "Dear Brother Tom." What followed was an amazing testimony of God's grace. Tom had gone on to become assistant chief of police in Meridian and retired after twenty years of service. He had been very skeptical when he heard about my conversion and subsequent call to ministry. As he put it, "For years I heard 'Tarrants is a preacher now.' Myself, being a play-like Christian at this time and not believing a person can change his life in this magnitude, could only say, 'Yeah, right, I'm sure he is.'"

But Tom's skepticism had faded. He wrote, "I spent the first forty-five years or so of my life playing at being a good Baptist. Then, some sixteen years ago I met and married my wife, Bonnie, not knowing that her background as a Pentecostal preacher's kid would persuade her to attempt to insure that this ole Baptist boy was saved." He concluded, saying he'd like to "meet for a cup of coffee and a long talk" and hoped I could come speak at his church someday.

A couple of emails and a few weeks later, Assistant Chief Tom Tucker and I met for that cup of coffee and long talk. It was quite a reunion, considering that the last time we had seen each other, we were locked in a blazing gun battle. Now there was no animosity or tension between us, just a comfortable friendliness.

We talked about where we were in life. We talked openly about how profoundly grateful we were that God had miraculously spared us from killing each other on that fateful night in Meridian. Neither of us could explain it any other way. We acknowledged how grateful we were to be alive and in a better place. When we parted, it was as two brothers grateful to have been given new lives through Jesus Christ and now to be friends by God's amazing, reconciling grace. And we are still in communication today.

I enjoyed the years I spent serving at the church and working with the other co-pastor, the elders, and the rest of the team there. And I had seen encouraging growth in many lives, including my own. But after passing the age of fifty, I began to think more about the future. The road ahead of me was going to be a lot shorter than the one behind. How could I give God my best in the time I had left? For years, I had wanted to do further study that could help me grow deeper in my own spiritual life and equip me to be more effective in helping people mature in theirs. If I was going to do that, it would be now or never. I began to pray and seek counsel and came to believe that I should move forward. After more prayer and investigation, I applied for and was accepted into a doctoral program in Christian spirituality. In order to give myself fully to my studies, I stepped down from my role at the church and became a full-time student.

# MAKING SENSE OF IT ALL

At this point in life, I had experienced more than my share of surprises from God. His plan had taken me in directions I had never dreamed of. And he wasn't finished. The greatest and most rewarding surprise was yet to come.

My doctoral studies did not take all of my time, so I prayed and asked the Lord if he had anything else he wanted me to do. Immediately, the thought came into my mind to contact Art Lindsey, president of the C. S. Lewis Institute in Washington, founded in 1976 by James Hiskey and Dr. James Houston. The institute's mission focused on equipping laypeople to live and share their faith in Christ in public and personal life as C. S. Lewis had done. This took the form of discipleship of heart and mind. The institute was nondenominational and committed to biblical orthodoxy. The ethos was "Unity in the essentials, liberty in the nonessentials, and love in all things." The inaugural lecturers were John R. W. Stott, J. I. Packer, and James Montgomery Boice, and leaders of their stature had been regular lecturers ever since. I met with Art for lunch a couple of times, and out of our conversations he suggested that I consider doing some volunteer work with the institute in the area of discipleship. I agreed.

Several months later, however, in September 1998, amid a worsening financial situation, the board of directors of the institute was considering closing their doors. But the ministry had been fruitful and seemed more needed than ever. Much to my surprise, Art proposed that they keep the doors open and call me to take over as president. Amazingly, the board unanimously agreed to take a step of faith and invite me to become president. They asked me to strengthen the institute's focus on discipleship and to make a commitment to remain in the position long enough for that goal to become a reality. This wasn't exactly what I was expecting as I happily worked on my doctoral studies. But after much prayer and counsel from family and friends close to me, it seemed clear that God was calling me to it. I accepted the mission and committed to stay for at least ten years.

The board's decision was unusual. Whatever qualifications one might expect for president of the institute, former terrorist and ex-convict were probably not among them. And given the financial condition, the critical role of the president in raising money, and my dislike for fund-raising, it made no sense at all. Yet at fifty-two years old, I committed at least the next ten years of my life to this ministry, which did much of its work quietly, serving area churches, pastors, and individuals. In time, this work would fulfill my dream of serving in a ministry focused on discipleship training and spiritual mentoring that would help strengthen the church. And it would turn out to be very compatible with my studies, though it would take a good deal longer to complete them and graduate.

When I started at the institute, the situation looked hopeless from a human perspective. It was just me and the former president, and our monthly donations were barely enough to pay the bills. I had never done anything like this before and was in over my head. I needed to pray a lot and to trust God to show us what he wanted to do and to provide what was needed to do it. To see God respond to prayer again and again over the years was inspiring and faith building. And to see him resurrect a ministry that was nearly dead was an incredible privilege. Additional volunteers were drawn to the team, giving much-needed help as we grew, and funding increased. Amazingly, God did all this in spite of that fact that I made plenty of mistakes along the way due to inexperience and ineptitude. It was very much a case of what God said to Paul, "my power is made perfect in weakness" (2 Cor 12:9). To compensate in areas where I was weak or deficient, God brought new staff with strong gifts and experience.

As I pondered why the Lord was doing this, I knew it wasn't because of us. I concluded that because of God's intention to restore authentic discipleship to his beleaguered church, he was raising up ministries like ours and others for that purpose. From one office in the Washington, DC, area, we have grown to seventeen cities in the United States and four other countries—and we are still growing.

Some surprises are good, but others are not so good. One day I got a phone call from Frank Watts. Our friendship had deepened over the years through periodic visits, phone calls, and walking together through the illness and death of his wife, Joyce, and the tragic death of his youngest son, at whose memorial service I had officiated. Frank told me he had cancer and asked for prayer support. Our phone calls became more frequent.

As his condition worsened, I made a trip to see him, one we both knew would be the last. I returned to Washington, DC, with a heavy heart. On his final day in this world, Frank called again. He was weak, and we didn't really talk much except to say that we loved each other and looked forward to seeing each other again in heaven. We prayed together and thanked God for our friendship. Then we said our goodbyes. It was a hard and very sad moment, but we both knew that death was not the final word and that there was a glorious future ahead.

\*     \*     \*

Through my work at the institute, I have occasionally spoken to groups about how God brought me to him. The most surprising event in all my years of public speaking occurred one night in my hometown of Mobile, Alabama, in 2007. I had been invited to speak at a midweek dinner at Springhill Presbyterian Church. As I was finishing my remarks, delivered in the church fellowship hall, a man in the audience stood up and identified himself as one of the Jewish boys I had roughed up and threatened when I was in high school. The church audience went dead silent. The tension was so thick you could almost cut it with a knife.

While everyone held their breath, Stan recounted for the entire audience how one day as we were passing in a hall between classes, I said to him, "You bastard kike!" And then he blurted, "You grabbed me by the throat, threw me up against the wall, and looked into my eyes with a hatred that burned bright and told me, 'The next time I see you, I am going to kill you.'" He related how he had struggled with fear, anger, hatred, and loathing for more than forty years. He recounted that a few weeks earlier, during Yom Kippur, he was praying hard for forgiveness of his sins, and my name came to his mind. He felt that he was being directed to forgive me and also to ask my forgiveness for hating me for more than forty years.

Then he walked toward me and said, "That is what I have come here tonight to do—to tell you that I forgive you, and to ask you to forgive me."

It was a very courageous act.

People at their tables were stunned. I was stunned. I stepped forward to meet him, and we shook hands and embraced. I told him I was sorry, assured him of my forgiveness, and asked him to forgive me. The barriers were broken down, and we began a new chapter in life.

Whose sin was greater, mine or his? Mine, of course, for creating the offense. But the good news is that God provided atonement for all of our sins through Christ's death on the cross, an atonement freely offered to everyone! And God can bring reconciliation between people no matter how far apart they may be. No matter how deeply we have sinned, no matter how much of a mess we have made of our lives, God invites us to turn to him and receive forgiveness and a new life through Jesus, his Son. There is no sin too great for God to forgive, no bondage too hard for him to break, no problem too difficult for him to solve. As Corrie ten Boom, who survived a Nazi death camp, said so well, "There is no pit so deep that God's love is not deeper still."[1]

I had been at the institute about twelve years when God interrupted my routines with an unexpected turn of events. In the midst of a very full work schedule, Derek, a young Chinese man I was mentoring in our C. S. Lewis Fellows program, asked me to preach at his church, where he was part of the leadership team. It was a congregation of young professionals, about half of whom were Chinese and the other half Korean, and nearly all were between twenty-two and thirty-two years old. He had asked me before, but I had declined, thinking I would be out of place in an Asian American church. My only exposure to Asian people had been on a mission trip to Korea, Singapore, Hong Kong, and mainland China back in the 1980s. But the invitation this time was different. His pastor had left to start a church in another state, and they needed a guest preacher on short notice. After praying about it, I agreed, not sure of what I was getting myself into.

Sometimes God calls us to leave our comfort zones because he wants to take us somewhere that's even better. That was the case here. After the first sermon, they asked me to preach for two more weeks. I was so busy that I should have said no. But they were zealous for God, hungry for his Word, and eager to serve him. They were also very friendly, winsome, and easy to love. The combination was irresistible, and I agreed.

Then they asked me to preach each Sunday for two months in order to give them enough time to interview the final candidates for the new pastor position. This was a much more challenging request. Preparing an expository sermon each week for that long was nearly impossible, because it would require at least fifteen to twenty hours of preparation. But they were a praying church and promised to intercede for me. To my amazement and great delight, I found that I was able to prepare a good sermon each week, even though it took every waking moment of the week outside of my daily work schedule.

As the two months drew to a close, the pastoral search committee said they needed more time. They asked if I would consider serving as interim pastor until they could find the right person to serve as their next pastor. If the two-month stretch made no sense, this made even less. But these guys had grown on me. I loved them and didn't want to leave them in the lurch. As I served there month after month, I found myself loving these brothers and sisters more and more and getting more involved in their needs—pastoral care, counseling, baptisms, and so on. Somehow, by God's grace, it all worked. What had seemed unthinkable at the beginning turned out to be a much-needed help to the church and one of the best times of ministry in my life, and the bonds of love and affection have continued.

*     *     *

The God of the Bible is a God of purpose and planning. He doesn't do things in a random or haphazard way. He is the greatest strategic master planner in the universe. And he especially likes to save and transform "nobodies" and use them for his glory. The prophet Amos was a farmer and herdsman. Jesus' first disciples, Peter, Andrew, James, and John, were fishermen—good, solid, blue-collar people. Before meeting Christ, the apostle Paul was a violent religious extremist. Augustine was a sex-addicted intellectual. Francis of Assisi was a rich playboy with no purpose in life. More recently, Chuck Colson was a ruthless Washington lawyer and political operative. These better-known examples stand out, but the bigger story is the countless nobodies over the centuries who are not recorded in the history books but were deeply changed by God's grace and became faithful servants of Jesus in their time.

I can see something of God's purposes in saving a nobody like me and leading me the way he has over the years. He had specific purposes and plans for my life, as he does for each of his children, and he calls us to step into them in faith and watch him work. As we do, our life stories turn out to be not so much about us as about God and his amazing grace.

In hindsight, I can see how at least part of his plan so far has been to deliver me from cheap grace and the racist, anti-Semitic ideology and political extremism that had ensnared me; and give me a passion for true grace, authentic discipleship, and living a life of love for God and others. I can also see that the ministry opportunities he has given me and the seemingly random relationships that have come into my life actually have an inner coherence and purpose. They have been chances to quietly love others and demonstrate the reconciling power of the gospel. And this is what he wants all believers to do.

When we embrace God's purposes and plans with the obedience of faith, he is glorified, and we are blessed. When we ignore or reject them, we suffer loss. One of the great keys to a blessed life is to fully surrender to God, ask him to fulfill his purposes for our lives, follow where he leads, and to keep on surrendering and following to our life's end.

We will not always get it right. Certainly, I haven't. My sins and stupidities testify against me. But God is not a demanding taskmaster; he is a loving and gracious Father who forgives and restores those who repent and return to him. He also gives us new chances to embrace his purposes and plans for our lives. He's the God of the second chance, the third chance, and many more.

# CONCLUSION

The Challenge We Face Today

We live in troubled times. The swirling vortex of social and political change afoot reminds me in some ways of the 1960s, leading me to a deepening concern about our racial, ethnic, and political divisions. These are serious social issues in their own right, but also serious discipleship issues for the church.

How Christians respond to these issues has major implications for the wider world and for the church. To respond properly, we must resist fear, anger, confusion, and hopelessness, and instead look to God in hope because nothing is impossible with him. And we must cry out to him in faith to do great and mighty things in our day, just as he has done in difficult times in the past.

Some may wonder why I say that racial, ethnic, and political divisions are serious discipleship issues for the church. It is because these issues (and a good many others) are actually symptoms of a deeper underlying problem in our personal and corporate lives as believers. That problem is the failure to live as Jesus calls us to live—under his total lordship over our lives. Unless we deal with this foundational issue—and its application to these concerns—we will continue to go around in circles.

I want to focus on how believers can face today's challenges in a way that is faithful to Jesus and glorifies God. I am not a political person and do not write about these things with a political agenda. Rather, I am someone who is trying to follow Jesus as best I can and who writes through the lens of his understanding of the Bible. The fundamental issue here is one of loving our neighbors as Jesus calls us to do. My hope is that this effort will encourage other followers of Jesus to think clearly and biblically about these issues and to publicly demonstrate the life-changing power of his gospel. If we do, God will be honored and people will be drawn to consider Christ's claims.

For this to happen, we must recognize that love and its fruits are absolutely essential for any credibility with the watching world. As Francis Schaeffer wrote, after admonishing believers to study issues and give honest answers, "After we have done our best to communicate to a lost world, still we must never forget that the final apologetic which Jesus gave is the observable love of true Christians for true Christians."[1] If we do not love one another, how can we expect the world to take us and the Savior we proclaim seriously?

Sadly, Christians are not generally noted for such love in today's world. Nor are we especially noted for loving nonbelievers. Of course, there have been times when Christians have been known for their joyful love for one another and their compassionate care for the lost, and this has had a powerful impact. As Sheldon Vanauken observed, "The best argument for Christianity is Christians: their joy, their certainty, their completeness. But the strongest argument against Christianity is also Christians—when they are somber and joyless, when they are self-righteous and smug in complacent consecration, when they are narrow and repressive, then Christianity dies a thousand deaths."[2] To that list, we might also add, "when they are seduced by racial and ethnic prejudice and extreme political ideology (whether left or right)."

If we are to recover our credibility as witnesses of Christ, we must first recover our love. How can we do so? First and foremost, we must answer the summons of Jesus Christ, who calls us to "seek first the kingdom of God and his righteousness" (Matt. 6:33), regardless of the cost (Mark 8:34–38, Luke 14:25–33).[3] God wants our wholehearted devotion and obedience; he wants to be supreme in our lives.

What does that look like? Jesus summed it up in the great commandment: love God supremely and love others sacrificially (Matt. 22:34–40). The first part is rooted in a desire to please the One who loves us and takes the form of grateful obedience to God for his grace and love in our lives. The second part takes the form of servant love for fellow believers, nonbelievers, and even enemies (Matt. 5:43–48). This mandate reaches across all the barriers that separate people—including race, ethnicity, culture, social class, economics, political convictions, and other allegiances. Yet given our current context, it is especially important to look at the implications for the great commandment in three particular areas: race, ethnicity, and political polarization.

## Racial Harmony

When Jesus ministered to the Samaritan woman at the well, he demonstrated the call to love people across racial and religious barriers (John 4:1–42). We can say this because the Samaritans were a mixed race with unorthodox beliefs.[4] Jesus made this call even clearer in the parable of the Good Samaritan. John Stott noted, "The main point of the parable of the Good Samaritan is its racial twist. It is not just that neighbor love ignores racial and national barriers, but that in Jesus' story, the Samaritan did for a Jew what no Jew would ever have dreamed of doing for a Samaritan."[5]

Jesus makes this even more explicit in the Great Commission (Matt. 28:18–20), when he sends out his followers to make disciples of "all nations." (In the Greek, *panta ta ethne* means every ethnic group, all the peoples of the earth.)

Racial and ethnic division and conflict is found worldwide. In America the well-known conflict between white and black people has a long and tragic history. And Christians, as well as nonbelievers, have been a part of this history. Many white Christians have been blind to our sinful attitudes toward people of other races, notably black people, and have failed to love them as Jesus taught us to do. And we have failed grievously in areas like slavery and Jim Crow laws and the civil rights movement.

The broader context of these failures among Christians is the subversion of biblical faith to culture, a subversion continuously at work all around us (and has been since the fall). When you combine that with our self-seeking, fallen nature (the flesh), the schemes of the devil, and the low level of spiritual transformation in most believers, you have a recipe for real trouble.

In terms of race, consider the ease with which we absorb and perpetuate racial attitudes of parents, families, and the sub-cultures in which we grow up. We do this unconsciously, for those attitudes are simply part of the air we breathe. When those attitudes are godly, this can be good and positive. But when they are not—when they are shaped by powerful, unrecognized values of the fallen world—we end up with a very different story. Such worldly values and attitudes can shape us, our churches, institutions, and the social structures in which we live (which is a longer discussion). They can also distort our understanding of the Bible and its demands upon us by coloring our reading of the scriptures with lenses that filter out the things we don't want to see or deal with or that conflict at a deeper level with unrecognized presuppositions. And when these dynamics dominate a church, pastors can be reluctant to challenge blindness and sin for fear of precipitating a church split or losing their job—or simply as a result of not knowing how to deal with the fallout in a redemptive way. These are just a few of the factors feeding the racial blindness that has been and continues to be passed down from generation to generation.

Recognizing and addressing these things is not as easy as we might think. We all have blind spots, and we are also much less logical and consistent than we like to imagine. And many of these things are so baked into our lives that it doesn't occur to us to examine them in any significant way. We can also be quite resistant to self-knowledge that challenges deeply entrenched issues we don't want to deal with. To a great extent, we are creatures of our times and culture. But there is hope—and a way out—as we will see ahead.

What must we do? Anyone who has received God's grace, been born of the Spirit, and who loves Jesus Christ must take seriously his command to love our neighbors. And to do so not only "in word or talk but in deed and in truth" (1 John 3:18). In other words, through concrete actions. When the world sees believers living in relationships of love that surmount the barriers that divide the nonbelieving world, it will witness striking evidence of God's supernatural power in action. As a result Jesus will be glorified, the gospel will gain fresh credibility and the great commission can progress. On the other hand, if our walk is not consistent with our talk, we forfeit our credibility. People are not stupid; they will not believe the message unless they trust the messenger. The recovery of trust is one of the great challenges facing the worldwide church today.

Billy Graham, though not perfect, was ahead of his time on the issue of race. His eyes began to be opened as early as 1952, when he determined that he would never again preach to a segregated audience and personally took down the ropes separating blacks and whites at one of his crusades. Graham highlighted this problem forcefully, and his observation about it is important to read in its entirety:

> Racial and ethnic hostility is the foremost social problem facing our world today.... Racism—in the world and in the church—is one of the greatest barriers to world evangelization....
>
> Racial and ethnic hatred is a sin, and we need to label it as such. Jesus told his disciples to "love your neighbor as yourself" (Matthew 22:39); and in reply to the question "Who is my neighbor?" he responded with a pointed parable about a good Samaritan, a member of a despised race (Luke 10:25–37).
>
> Racism is a sin precisely because it keeps us from obeying God's command to love our neighbor, and because it has its roots in pride and arrogance. Christians who harbor racism in their attitudes or actions are not following Jesus at this point, for Christ came to bring reconciliation—reconciliation between us and God, and reconciliation between each other. He came to accept us as we are, whoever we are, "from every tribe and language and people and nation (Revelation 5:9)."[6]

Any racial or ethnic prejudice in our lives indicates that we are compromising the teachings of Christ, which can undermine the credibility of the gospel itself. But it doesn't have to be this way. The church can and should take moral leadership in society by embracing biblical principles and resources on race. Even if it doesn't, individual believers like you and me can. We have the power to overcome our prejudices and love people who are different from us "because God's love has been poured into our hearts through the Holy Spirit who has been given to us" (Rom. 5:5). All we need is the desire and a willing heart. And if we lack this, we should ask God to give it to us. If we are serious, he will.

Given all of this, what are some *concrete* steps we can take to move forward in love?

Just as children must crawl before they can walk, and walk before they can run, we must start with the basics. What follows are baby steps, because that is where I believe many people are on these issues. First, do a prayerful self-examination (Ps. 139:23–24). Ask God to open your eyes to your sins, especially sinful attitudes toward people of other races and backgrounds. Such attitudes are found all over the world, so we should not be surprised if we discover them in ourselves. To root out these attitudes and their negative baggage, it is essential to begin by confessing and repenting of them before God. John Stott's words are helpful to ponder:

> I dare say that no man is altogether free from some taint of racial pride, because no man is free from sin. A sense of racial superiority is natural to us all, even if it is secret and undiscovered. Further, there is a black racism and well as a white. Everyone assumes that his race and colour are the norm, and that others are the abnorm, the deviation. This is simply the self-centredness of sin. But there is no norm in the colour of human skin, any more than there is in the colour of bird plumage. The norm is humanity: the races are variants of this. This means that all forms of racism are wrong. They are an offence against God, the God of creation and history, of religion, nature and judgment.[7]

Next, explore race-related themes and get some perspective by reading a book or two or other resources that foster in-depth thinking.[8] Doing so can provide a clearer understanding of the issues, giving us truth and reality about the effects of race and ethnicity on people who are different from us. It is also important to reflect on some of the longstanding attitudes and values toward minorities that are still embedded in our culture, as well as the way various social systems impact those who are outside of the dominant culture. As you do, ask God to show you what he wants you to see and to do next. Acting on the truth we learn is essential for spiritual growth. Failure to do so leads us into self-deception (James 1:22–25).

Then, pray for God to give you at least one friend of another race and help you build an open, honest relationship with no agenda other than love and the friendship it produces. Building friendships of any kind in our highly individualistic, isolating culture is a challenge and takes commitment. But it is well worth the effort and can open your eyes and enrich your life in ways that nothing else can. Such friendship can produce surprising fruit, as Billy Graham discovered. Dr. Martin Luther King Jr. said, "Had it not been for the ministry of my good friend, Dr. Billy Graham, my work in the civil rights movement would not have been as successful as it has been."[9]

Let the relationship grow at its own pace. As it does, seek to learn and to build trust. Learn about your new friend's life—what has shaped him, his joys and sorrows, hopes and dreams, his past and present challenges. Then share your story with him, doing so in a natural way, not a forced or artificial way.

Race will come up at some point as the relationship unfolds. When it does, discuss your respective experiences. If you have built trust, the conversation can take you into places you may know little about. Learning what it is like to walk in the other person's shoes will open up new vistas of understanding you've never considered before.

Friendships were the key for me and opened my eyes to many things of which I was completely unaware. I was surprised at how clueless I was about things that were very basic. Like most white people in America, I didn't have much understanding of other races. One of the main reasons for this is actually quite simple: white people have been the majority and dominant race in America since its founding. We have lived in our own culture and have not needed to learn much, if anything, about people from minority cultures. We have also made the rules and they make sense to us, even if they don't to others. Thus, the white culture tends to be unaware of many important things in the respective cultures of African Americans, Hispanics, Asians, and others. Even if our intentions are good, we don't know what we don't know. And this blindness—willful or not—produces false assumptions about people, faulty perceptions of problems and issues, and damaging blunders in relationships. At the same time, people from minority cultures in America have had to live in two cultures: their own plus the dominant white culture, so they see and understand a lot that is not obvious to whites. If we whites will take the posture of learners, we can learn a lot from others and potentially make progress in developing friendly, harmonious relationships with people of different races and ethnic groups.

Pastors should, of course, lead the way in this, setting an example for their congregations. Jesus led by example and so must his followers. But whether pastors take the initiative or not, every follower of Jesus should prayerfully step out in faith, trusting God to lead and direct and give the wisdom needed. Even a casual reading of the Bible shows that God has done this for centuries; he is still doing it today and wants to use us as conduits of his healing power.

## Anti-Semitism

As with racism, conduct a prayerful self-examination to discover and deal with any anti-Semitic ideas, attitudes, or stereotypes you may have picked up. It is obvious that Christians should have an appreciation for and love of the Jewish people and seek their good. We are greatly indebted to them for the Scriptures, and from them came Jesus the Messiah and the apostles. We also need to realize that God has good plans for them that are yet to be fulfilled (Rom. 11:1–36). If you find any traces of anti-Semitism in your heart, confession and repentance are the starting point and should be followed by working through whatever issues you need to address.

In addition, do some reading about anti-Semitism and its history, which is very well-known to Jewish people but apart from the Holocaust is little known by most non-Jews.[10] Among the discoveries Christians will make is the fact that those who I call "pseudo-Christians" have been responsible for much persecution of the Jews and in some cases terrible slaughters of Jewish people in Europe over the centuries. Perhaps more shocking are deeply troubling anti-Semitic comments by those we regard as true Christians—leaders like Augustine and John Chrysostom. Even worse are Martin Luther's anti-Semitic diatribes against the Jews, which were used by the Nazis to justify the Holocaust. This history reveals something of the complexity of how Christians have related to Jewish people.

Again, relationships are crucial, so look for friends of Jewish descent. Friendships with Jewish people have been helpful to me, especially those who have found Jesus as their Messiah. Let the relationship grow at its own pace. Learn about your friend's life—what has shaped him, his joys and sorrows, hopes and dreams, and his current challenges. Ask about his religious beliefs—what he believes about God and the Bible. Some Jews believe in the God of the Hebrew Bible, others are agnostics, and still others are atheists.

Also ask what it has been like to be Jewish in a Gentile world. Part of the history of Gentile anti-Semitism is the forced conversion of Jews by the church on pain of death or expulsion, which began as early as the 400s in the Middle East and continued up to the nineteenth century in Europe. Every Jewish person is painfully aware of this. If you have built trust, it will open the door into a place you know little, if anything, about. Just listen and learn. Where appropriate, express your sorrow at what he has experienced, because there will likely be plenty of hurt.

Feel free to share the story of how Christ's life, death, and resurrection have affected you. If your friend asks questions, feel free to answer him. But do not push. That will only raise barriers. Make sure to communicate that your friendship does not depend on him coming to share your faith, but that you share it out of love. Also bear in mind that with Jews, as with all people, professions of friendship and love mean little unless they are accompanied by concrete acts of love. In one of our conversations, Al Binder, the Jewish lawyer who encouraged my release from prison, said to me, "try to do something to help the Jews, if you can." This book and the earlier ones I wrote, as well as frequent warnings to Christians about the dangers of anti-Semitism, have been part of my response.

If you will take the very basic relational steps described above—seeking to please God and trusting in him—he will empower, guide, direct, and teach you. And he will give you further light when you are ready for it.

## Political Polarization

Seeking the common good and loving people across political divides can seem intimidating in this highly contentious period. Why should we even make the effort? Because God calls us to love our neighbor and seek his or her good (even when our neighbor is an enemy, Matt.5:43–48). How can we engage with people whose political views and values are very different from our own? Three things are essential: the desire for a relationship, a serious effort to build bridges, and an attitude of graciousness. We must relate to others in a Christlike way—with love, humility, gentleness, patience, and respect. If we lack any of these, we can ask God to give them to us.

For a Christian, it is not an option to dismiss people with whom we disagree as beyond hope, a threat to the public good, or even simply not worth our time and attention. If the person is a fellow Christian, we are called to seek peace and unity as much as possible. If the person is not a Christian, we must remember that no one is beyond the reach of God's love and grace. If God can save people on the Far Right like I once was, he can save people on the Far Left and anywhere else on the political spectrum! If we are Christians, we must take seriously Jesus' call to love not only our neighbors but also our enemies. Jesus explicitly rejected the commonly held idea that we should hate our enemies (Matt. 5:43–48). No matter how much we may disagree with someone, we must treat that person with courtesy and seek to reason with them, building a respectful relationship and finding common ground where possible.

There are things about which reasonable people can agree and things about which reasonable people can disagree. Or, to put it slightly differently, we can disagree agreeably. There is no justification for hating those who think differently from us. And hating doesn't just mean violent dislike. It is just as frequently expressed as ostracism, ridicule, rejection, and malice. To be clear, building respectful relationships does not require compromising one's convictions. It just requires good will, civility, and obedience to God, who calls his people to "turn away from evil and do good; seek peace and pursue it" (Ps. 34:14). And obedience to God includes faithfully following Jesus, who sends us out to be peacemakers (Matt. 5:9) in the church and the world—and not people who foment strife and division.

Discussing politics is perfectly appropriate, as are efforts to convince others of our point of view. But we must keep in mind that the *highest* priority for a Christian is not to change a person's political views but to help change their eternal destiny if they don't know Christ. Getting into contentious arguments about their politics will only hinder your efforts. When you discuss politics with anyone, whether a believer or nonbeliever, it should not be with an underlying anger and hostility, but in friendly dialog and with a humble, irenic spirit. And also with an ability to state their positions in a way that they agree is accurate. Without such clarity about the other person's views, little, if any, progress can be made. Regardless of differences, seek to become a friend—get to know the other person as a person. Seek to understand something of their life, what has influenced them, what is important to them, and why they think as they do. And be patient. Love is patient and kind and can open the doors of friendship like nothing else can, but it takes time.

Obviously, the suggestions I have offered above are not hardball politics. Some people will think that such an approach is hopelessly naive or compromising and is doomed to failure. But that line of thinking does not recognize that our current crisis is ultimately a spiritual problem, not just a social or political one. Yes, we must address the social and political dimensions; that is certainly necessary. But it is not sufficient. Ultimately, we must look to God and his supernatural power to change people, to revive the church, and to bring moral and social reform—something which he has done again and again over the centuries.[11] Zerubbael was told that victory would come "not by might, nor by power, but by my Spirit says the Lord of hosts" (Zech. 4:6).

Let us then not give in to fear, anger, or hopelessness but go forward in faith, hope, and love, trusting our sovereign, all-powerful God. And let us live as faithful witnesses of Jesus Christ, loving our neighbors, sharing the gospel and seeking to be grace-filled peacemakers, and remembering that Jesus is with us every step of the way.

# ACKNOWLEDGMENTS

I want to express my deep appreciation to the board of the C. S. Lewis Institute for granting me a sabbatical leave to work on this book. I also want to thank the colleagues and friends who supported me in this work through prayer, finances, and helpful comments on the manuscript at various stages. To the friend who helped me first put this story into print, profound thanks. And thanks to the wonderful editors who helped me bring it up-to-date!

# NOTES

## Chapter 4: Seeds of Fear and Anger

1. George Wallace, inaugural address, Montgomery, Alabama, January 14, 1963, online at http://digital.archives.alabama.gov/cdm/ref/collection/voices/id/2952.
2. Douglas Martin, "Nicholas Katzenbach, 90, Dies; Policy Maker at '60s Turning Points," *New York Times*, May 9, 2012, https://www.nytimes.com/2012/05/10/us/nicholas-katzenbach-1960s-political-shaper-dies-at-90.html.

## Chapter 5: Descending into Darkness

1. Adolf Hitler, *Mein Kampf*, vol. 1, chap. 6, online at http://www.hitler.org/writings/Mein_Kampf/mkv1ch06.html.
2. Tom Stafford, "How Liars Create the 'Illusion of Truth,'" BBC Future, October 26, 2016, http://www.bbc.com/future/story/20161026-how-liars-create-the-illusion-of-truth.
3. Eric Hoffer, *The True Believer: Thoughts on the Nature of Mass Movements* (New York: Harper & Row, 1951).
4. John White, *The Cost of Commitment* (Downers Grove, IL: InterVarsity Press, 2006), 43.

## Chapter 6: Opening Skirmishes

1. C.S. Lewis, *Mere Christianity* (New York: Touchstone Editions, 1996), 87.

### Chapter 9: Prison Life

1. Mariel Alper, Matthew R. Durose, and Joshua Markman, "2018 Update on Prisoner Recidivism: A 9-Year Follow-Up Period (2005–2014)," Bureau of Justice Statistics, May 23, 2018, https://www.bjs.gov/index.cfm?ty =pbdetail&iid=6266.

### Chapter 12: Maximum Security—Again

1. Rev. John Henry Hanson, "Saint Monica and the Child of Her Tears," St. Josemaria Institute, August 23, 2016, https://stjosemaria.org /saint-monica-child-of-her-tears/.

### Chapter 13: Encounter with Truth and Light

1. George Charles Roche, *Legacy of Freedom* (New Rochelle, NY: Arlington House, 1969), 20–21.
2. James Burnham, *Suicide of the West* (New York: Encounter Books, 1964), 100–101.
3. Burnham, 103–4.
4. Burnham, 103.
5. Charles Wesley (1707–1788), "And Can It Be That I Should Gain."

### Chapter 14: New Life!

1. John Newton (1725–1807), "Amazing Grace."
2. Francis Schaeffer, *The Francis A. Schaeffer Trilogy: The Three Essential Books in One Volume*, bk. 1, *The God Who Is There* (Wheaton, IL: Crossway Books, 1990), 165.
3. Thomas Williams, "Saint Anselm," *The Stanford Encyclopedia of Philosophy* (spring 2016 ed.), ed. Edward N. Zalta, https://plato.stanford .edu/archives/spr2016/entries/anselm/.
4. 2 Chronicles 33:1–16.
5. Acts 9:1–19.
6. John Newton, *The Amazing Works of John Newton* (Alachua, FL: Bridge-Logos, 2009), 338.
7. Aleksandr Solzhenitsyn, quoted in Daniel Mahoney, *Aleksandr Solzhenitsyn: The Ascent from Ideology* (Lanham, MD: Rowman & Littlefield, 2001), 50.
8. "The More Than 100 Million Deaths that Communism Caused, Divided by Countries," *Counting Stars* (blog), December 18, 2017, http://www

.outono.net/elentir/2017/12/18/the-more-than-100-million-deaths-that
-communism-caused-divided-by-countries/.

9. C. S. Lewis, "They Asked for a Paper," in *Is Theology Poetry?* (London: Geoffrey Bless, 1962), 164–65.

10. Source unknown.

11. Thomas à Kempis, *Of the Imitation of Christ: In Four Books*, new ed. (New York: Frederick A. Stokes & Brother, 1889), 293.

## Chapter 16: New Possibilities

1. "Hoover and the FBI," PBS, accessed February 12, 2019, http://www.pbs .org/hueypnewton/people/people_hoover.html.

## Chapter 18: Ole Miss: A Happy Change

1. St. Augustine of Hippo, *The Confessions of St. Augustine* (Ger.: Jazzybee Verlag, n.d.), 58.

## Chapter 19: A New Direction

1. Mark Twain, *The Innocents Abroad* (first edition, 1869), 243.

2. Twain, *The Innocents Abroad*, 243.

3. About a year after I left, the School for Urban Missions folded.

## Chapter 20: Making Sense of It All

1. Corrie ten Boom, *The Hiding Place* (Grand Rapids, MI: Chosen, 2006), 8.

## Conclusion

1. Francis Schaeffer, *The Mark of a Christian* (Downers Grove, IL: InterVarsity Press, 2006), 29.

2. Sheldon Vanauken, *A Severe Mercy* (New York: Harper & Row, 1977), 82.

3. John White, *The Cost of Commitment* (Downers Grove, IL: InterVarsity Press, 2006); also, Dietrich Bonhoeffer, *The Cost of Discipleship* (New York: Touchstone, 1995).

4. The hatred between Jews and Samaritans was comparable to that between white racists and black people during America's worst days.

5. John Stott, *Issues Facing Christians Today* (London: Collins/Marshall Pickering, 1990), 140.

6. "Billy Graham on Racism," The Billy Graham Library, January 8, 2018, https://billygrahamlibrary.org/billy-graham-racism/.

7. John Stott, *Racialism v. Our Common Humanity*, Church of England Newspaper, May 10, 1968.

8. A good start would be: John Perkins, *Let Justice Roll Down* (Regal Books, 2006) and John Perkins, *One Blood* (Moody Publishers, 2018).

9. Kate Shellnutt, "What Is Billy Graham's Friendship with Martin Luther King Jr. Worth?," *Christianity Today*, February 23, 2018, https://www .christianitytoday.com/news/2018/february/billy-graham-martin-luther -king-jr-friendship-civil-rights.html. It should be noted that Dr. King wanted Billy Graham to be more active in publicly supporting the civil rights movement, but that Graham was concerned that doing so would close many doors to his evangelistic work.

10. For an initial orientation, see Joe Carter, "The FAQs: What Christians Should Know About Antisemitism," The Gospel Coalition, October 30, 2018, https://www.thegospelcoalition.org/article/the-faqs-what-christians -should-know-about-antisemitism/. Movies like *Schindler's List* and *The Hiding Place* can remind us of the realities of the Holocaust.

11. For example, through the eighteenth Evangelical Awakening in Britain and the work of such key figures as John Wesley, John Newton, William Wilberforce, the Clapham group, and people like Lord Shaftesbury and Hannah More.

# ABOUT THE AUTHOR

Thomas A. Tarrants is president emeritus of the C. S. Lewis Institute, where he served from 1998 to 2019. Prior to working at the institute, he was co-pastor of a multiracial church in Washington, DC. He is a member of the Evangelical Theological Society and is an ordained minister in the Evangelical Church Alliance. Tom has pursued a ministry of teaching, writing, and spiritual mentoring for many years, with a focus on discipleship, prayer, and devotional life. He holds a master of divinity degree and a doctor of ministry degree in Christian spirituality.